GOOD NEWS YOU CAN USE

40 Life-Changing Lessons and Stories of Hope and Joy That Will Encourage, Inspire, and Ignite Your Personal Faith-Fire!

JERRY KING

Copyright © 2024 Jerry King

ISBN: 9798329559521
Independently published

Printed in the United States of America
All rights reserved. No portion of this book may be reproduced, stored in a retrieval system, or transmitted in any form by any means - electronically, mechanical photocopy, recording, scanning, or other - except for brief quotations in critical reviews or articles, without the prior written permission of the publisher/author.

Scripture quotations marked NIV are from the Holy bible, New International Version*, NIV*. c 1973, 1978, 1984, 2011 by Biblica, Inc.* Used by permission of Zondervan. All rights reserved worldwide.

Italics added to Scripture quotations are the author's own emphasis.

Any internet addresses or company or product information printed in this book are offered as a resource and are not intended in any way to be or to imply and endorsement by the author, nor does the author vouch for the existence, content, or services of these sites beyond the life of this book.

DEDICATION

To Lucy

After over five decades of marriage, I am blessed and amazed at the depth of your patience and love. Your smile and laughter bring music to my life, and you've made me so very happy. Truly, you turned my heart inside out and showed me what love was about. I will always have an endless love, be stuck on you, and offer praise that we're still having fun and you're still the one. Most importantly, we both know that our love is eternal because Jesus Is Love!

(This includes the titles of several of our favorite songs. Always remember that I love you more today than yesterday—but not as much as tomorrow!)

Contents

Author's Personal Note　　　　　　　　　　　　　　　　　　　　iv

Section One: GAME CHANGERS!　　　　　　　　　　　　　　1
1. Pull a Weed and Plant a Seed　　　　　　　　　　　　　　　2
2. The Nitty-Gritty Greatness of Gratitude　　　　　　　　　　　6
3. If You Are Able – Come to the Table　　　　　　　　　　　　10
4. Too Blessed to Be Stressed　　　　　　　　　　　　　　　　14
5. Mistakes and Mess-Ups Make You a Masterpiece　　　　　　19
6. The Power of Purpose and Passion　　　　　　　　　　　　24
7. Now Get a REAL Life　　　　　　　　　　　　　　　　　　28
8. Broken and Restored Make Us Better Than Before　　　　　32
9. Magic, Myth or Miracle?　　　　　　　　　　　　　　　　36
10. Always on Time Every Time　　　　　　　　　　　　　　40
11. Pain Purifies Your Priorities　　　　　　　　　　　　　　　43
12. Face Your Fears and Defeat Defiant Giants　　　　　　　　47
13. Strong and Courageous Can Be Contagious　　　　　　　　51
14. Dealing with Difficult, Disagreeable People　　　　　　　　55
15. It's Hard to Be Humble When You're Perfect　　　　　　　60
16. Life's Toughest Tests Can Bring Out Your Best　　　　　　64
17. Real Living Begins with Forgiving　　　　　　　　　　　　68
18. Bloom Where You Are Planted　　　　　　　　　　　　　73
19. Staying Steady in Your Storms　　　　　　　　　　　　　77
20. Celebrate Laughter Through the Hereafter　　　　　　　　81
21. Radical Religion or Remarkable Relationship?　　　　　　86
22. Be a Dream Maker – Not a Heartbreaker　　　　　　　　　92
23. Rejuvenating Rest: Be Still and Just Chill　　　　　　　　　96

Section Two: GAME PLAN!   101
24. More Than Just a Book-of-the-Month   102
25. A Reason for Every Season   107
26. God's Top Ten Is the Perfect Place to Begin   111
27. Shy Sheep Need a Sharp-Minded Shepherd   115
28. Find Peace in the Pit and Never Quit   120
29. Different Names Mean the Same   124
30. A Lawyer Looking for a Loophole   129
31. He Can Inspire and Ignite Your Faith-Fire   133
32. Heavenly Hope Can Help You Cope   138
33. Note of Love from Above   143
34. One Main Rule in the Rabbi's School   147
35. 8 Ways to Be Blessed in A Mess   151
36. Pray This – Not That   155
37. The Salt Tastes Right and YOU Are the Light 160

Section Three: GAME TIME!   164
38. Trust the Son of Man with Your Life-Plan   165
39. Find Jubilant Joy on Your Life-Journey   170
40. Unleash Unlimited Love--Start Living Life Out Loud! 175

Digging Deeper – Small Group Study Guide   180
Gratitude   182
Bibliography, Sources, and Notes   183
Purchase and Contact Information   187
Notes & Quotes (Pages for reader's own notes) 188

Author's Personal Note

Everyone enjoys a good story and some of my favorites include children. Like the one about a little girl who has a small part as an angel in the church Christmas play. She would only be saying one line to the shepherds, "Behold, I bring you good tidings of great joy". But the adults told her it was a very important line, so she practiced it for hours with her parents.

Finally, her big moment arrived. She stood on the stage, looked at the sea of people with all their eyes focused on her, and you can imagine what happened next. The same thing many of us have experienced. Her mind went completely blank, and she couldn't remember a single word of the line she rehearsed.

She paused for a few seconds of awkward silence, then broke into an ear-to-ear smile and enthusiastically yelled, "Hey Guys! WOW–have I got some Good News for you!" Immediate standing ovation!

Good News: One of the meanings of *good tidings* in scripture is Good News. And the Greek word *gospel* also means good news or good message.

It is the most important, life-changing birth announcement in history. The Breaking News story that the Messiah has arrived so we can experience a full and abundant life!

You Can Use: Start applying these daily doses of Good News to your life beginning *today. Information plus inspiration and application equals transformation.*

You will learn or be reminded how to make positive changes and live a meaningful life–full of God's hope, love, peace and overflowing with joy.

40 Lessons and Stories: The number *40* has symbolic spiritual significance. In scriptures it often refers to a period of testing and learning, resulting in spiritual growth.

It rained 40 days and nights while Noah and his family were on the ark. Moses wandered in the wilderness for 40 years and Jesus spent 40 days in the desert. Jesus remained on earth 40 days after his resurrection and before His ascension.

I am excited and look forward to sharing life-lessons, stories, and spiritual insights with you. My prayer is you will be encouraged and most importantly be inspired to ignite your personal faith-fire!

Section 1: GAME-CHANGERS!

Game-Changers are those one or two special plays or situations that can literally determine the outcome of a game or competition.

In the game of life, it is those decisions and responses that determine whether we live a life of simply existing or one of lasting, eternal significance.

Section One focuses on real life situations—the thrill of victories and the agony of defeats that we all encounter. Each chapter includes relevant personal experiences and a brief summary or paraphrase of the main scripture passage—*Snapshot Picture of Scripture*. Highlights include personal insights regarding how Christ encourages, teaches, and reminds you how to love, laugh, and live a full and abundant life!

1

Pull a Weed and Plant a Seed

Standing on our back deck in total shock I shouted, "This is absolutely unbelievable." I tried to understand what happened. About a fourth of our once beautiful grass backyard had been plowed and cultivated to its current condition of brown, dry dirt.

A call to my dad quickly solved the mystery. He proudly confirmed he wanted to surprise Lucy and me so we could experience the 'fun and thrill' of growing and harvesting our own fresh vegetables.

I considered explaining that he grew up on a farm and I was clueless about anything relating to gardening or farming. But he was so excited I decided not to mention it.

He visited us a few weeks later but instead of a beautiful garden he saw a large area of dirt now overgrown and full of weeds.

In his calm, mentoring, father-to-son voice he shared his important *Gardening for Dummies* advice.

"It's really fairly simple," dad said, "You just pull a weed and plant a seed."

I wondered to myself, but didn't consider sharing, "Why don't you just go to the grocery store? Beans and corn really are not *that* expensive."

One of the most familiar stories in scripture about sowing and growing seeds is found in three of the four gospels.

Snapshot Picture of Scripture (Mark 4:1-9)

This passage is one of the first major accounts of Jesus' teaching the Good News. It is commonly known as the Parable of the Sower or Parable of the Soil.

A parable is simply a fictional, earthly story used to illustrate an eternal truth. When Jesus taught, He used common things like sheep, fish, bread, soil, vineyards, and salt to help listeners learn and remember his spiritual lessons.

He used parables more than any method of teaching. "Jesus spoke all these things to the crowd in parables; He did not say anything to them without using a parable" (Matthew 13:34 NIV).

In this parable of the soil, He shared about a farmer who sowed seed. The seed fell on one of four types of soil: hard, rocky, thorny, or good soil. It contains one of the foundational truths of how we are to receive and share the Good News of God's love.

He further explained that the seed represents God's Word. And the soil represents the condition of our hearts and how we receive and respond to the Good News.

Compare the different soils with our hearts:
1. Packed Path Heart–too hard to hear or see
2. Grainy Gravel Heart–shallow, no root growth
3. Worldly Weeds Heart–other things are more important
4. Good Ground Heart–prepared to receive, grow, and produce a crop. This is the type of heart Christ desires for each of us.

Messiah the Master Teacher

When most believers hear the name *Jesus*, familiar titles like Lord or Son of God quickly come to mind. But the Messiah was also known as the Master Teacher. Of the ninety times Jesus was addressed directly in the gospels, sixty times He was called Teacher or *rabbi*.

One of the things that differentiated Jesus from other rabbis is how His students were chosen. Many Jewish boys memorized the first five books of the law, the Torah, by around age 10. But some went on and memorized much of the entire Hebrew Bible, Tanakh, and were selected to be a rabbi's disciple.

But Jesus rocked the boat by going where His disciples worked–fishing or collecting taxes—and called them to follow Him.

And rabbi is how His disciples (students) referred to Him and the word the multitudes used. They were so amazed at His teaching because He taught with more authority than the other teachers of the law they were accustomed to hearing.

It's also the way Jesus referred to himself, "You call me teacher and Lord, and you are right, for that is what I am" (John 13:13 ESV).

Jesus the Master Teacher used simple stories to teach profound, life-changing lessons.

As an educator for most of my career, I was blessed with many opportunities to know, observe, and work with exceptional school leaders, staff, and teachers.

The most outstanding teachers demonstrated numerous traits, including in-depth knowledge of the subject, connecting new content with previous learning, hands-on projects, technology skills, a healthy sense of humor, and the ability to effectively communicate with their students using real world examples, stories and illustrations.

An additional characteristic that made Jesus such an exceptional rabbi was His compassion, empathy, and love for people. He perfectly demonstrated the expression, "People don't care how much you know until they know how much you care."

One of my most caring teachers was Mrs. Billig, my eighth grade Social Studies teacher. She sincerely cared about me and took the time to tell me. (Considering the challenging conduct I sometimes demonstrated in her class makes her especially memorable.)

It's all about getting the students' attention.

In an effort to get my rather rowdy high school students' attention during my first year as a teacher I decided that on the last day before Christmas break to dress up like Santa Claus. The students thought it was awesome and things were going great until about halfway through class.

My administrator walked in to see what kind of job the new teacher he hired was doing. His mouth fell open in disbelief as he observed me standing on top of my desk, dressed in a complete Santa Claus suit—including beard and boots—leading a class discussion. I vividly recall thinking, "Okay Jerry, since this teaching gig isn't going to work out, what is your Plan B for a second career?"

I reflect on how Jesus was such an amazing teacher who performed miracles and signs so people would listen to His life-changing message. He never entered a classroom, as we know a classroom, and never had an educational degree, as we understand a degree.

But the lesson plans He used to teach people literally changed their lives and eventually, changed the world. These same life-changing lessons recorded in scripture are available and applicable to us today!

At the core of Jesus' teaching the Good News are His references to the Kingdom of God, which He taught is here and now. It is mentioned fifty-three times in the gospels. Many of His parables pertained to the Kingdom, which began with his three years of ministry on earth.

With God's help we have the choice to change or cultivate our soil (hearts). We don't have to be stuck with who and what we currently are. We can be transformed by the humble acceptance and belief of the Good News. *How you care for your heart will determine the life you grow*!

This is an encouraging challenge and a profound promise. If you listen and cultivate your heart, the life God can bring in you, to you, and through you will be greater and more fulfilling than you can ever imagine!

This parable is for *you*!

Do you remember the true story about Johnny Appleseed? John Chapman loved apples so much he spent fifty years traveling around the country with bags of apple seeds, resulting in hundreds of orchards—some still around today.

Perhaps you recall a science class project when everyone received a cup with dirt and a seed. For several weeks you waited until a plant eventually broke through the soil and then watched it grow. Wherever you are in your faith journey, focus on a significant life-lesson from this parable—*the importance of spiritual growth*.

The Parable of the Sower and Soil was specifically chosen to start our trip together. I encourage you to read the words (receive the seeds) of the Good News with an open heart and mind (good soil) as we go and grow together. *So, pack your bags, buckle up, and let's go!*

Positive Points to Ponder
- Beginning today, look for someone in need and sow a heart-felt love-seed.
- Imagine the difference we could make in people's lives if we commit to daily sowing seeds of:
  —JOY in the midst of sorrow
  —PEACE in the midst of chaos
  —KINDNESS in the midst of cruelty
  —GOODNESS in the midst of selfishness
  —HOPE in the midst of giving up
  —LOVE in the midst of hate and indifference.

2

The Nitty-Gritty Greatness of Gratitude

Mealtimes at home were always interesting when my sister Ronda and I were growing up. We were expected to say the blessing before eating.

Admittedly, many times the words weren't even close to a sincere expression of gratitude. More like a requirement by our parents before we could enjoy one of mom's delicious, home-cooked meals.

The words were familiar: "God is great, God is good; let us thank Him for our food. By His hands we all are fed, thank you Lord for daily bread. Amen."

And if I was in a hurry and especially hungry, with one eye open it went something like: "Good veggies. Good meat. Thanks Lord. Let's eat!"

Not exactly from a heart of gratefulness. One of the most meaningful stories in scripture demonstrating gratitude, and the lack thereof, is the healing of ten lepers.

Snapshot Picture of Scripture (Luke 17:11-19)

Jesus was traveling to Jerusalem when He saw ten lepers. People diagnosed with leprosy during His lifetime were isolated from the rest of society into leper colonies. When people approached them the lepers were required by Jewish law to shout, "Unclean!"

It's interesting that instead of healing them immediately Jesus wanted to test their faith. So, He told the lepers to go present themselves to the priests—who could officially declare them healed.

How disappointing it must have been when only one out of the ten who were healed returned to Jesus to show gratitude and thank Him. What makes the situation even more intriguing is the one who thanked Him was a Samaritan, considered a half-breed outcast by the Jews.

It's easy to think, "How could the other nine be so ungrateful?" until we consider the missed opportunities we've personally experienced.

How to Go from Grumbling and Griping to Gratitude:
No amount of regret can change the past.
No amount of anxiety can change the future.
But *any* amount of gratitude can change the present.

It all begins with thoughts and *words*. As we were reminded in the parable of the soil, words are like seeds and our hearts and minds are like soil. When people complain and tear others down, negative seeds may be in their soil (hearts).

The Apostle Paul shares in his letter to the Philippians that we should 'do everything without grumbling'.

We can also make a choice in our own minds to begin a habit of expressing positive thankfulness to others for our blessings. *Pause and reflect on your personal blessings—especially the people for whom you are grateful.*

Perhaps you recall as a child at Thanksgiving tracing your hand on a sheet of paper, then drawing and coloring the picture of a turkey. Or listing as many words possible out of the word Thanksgiving.

Heartfelt gratitude helps us see God in our daily life—not just one time a year. It opens our spiritual eyes. There is a cycle of giving God thanks: *the more we express gratitude to Him and others, the more we see Him working with us and through us every day.*

Benefits of Giving and Living with Gratitude:
1. *Gratitude brings peace.* The apostle Paul shared, "Do not be anxious about anything, but in every situation, by prayer and thanksgiving, present your requests to God" (Philippians 4:6 NIV).
2. *Gratitude deepens our faith.* It is a faith-booster when we face tough times. God's record of being faithful to us is 100%. "Give thanks to the Lord, for He is good! His faithful love endures forever" (Psalm 136:1 NLT).
3. *Gratitude leads to joy and happiness.* When we realize God's goodness, it puts us on a daily path of joy. "The Lord has done great things for us, and we are filled with joy" (Psalm 126:3 NIV).

It's always the right moment to be grateful.
In happy moments—Praise God.
In difficult moments—Seek God.

> In quiet moments—Worship God.
> In painful moments—Trust God.
> In EVERY moment—Thank God!

In his book *Good to Great,* author Jim Collins tells the true story of Col. Charles Plumb that demonstrates gratitude in action. As a US Navy jet pilot in Vietnam, his plane was shot down and destroyed. After parachuting he was captured and somehow survived six years in a communist prison before he returned home.

One day Col. Plumb and his wife were sitting in a restaurant and a man who was sitting at another table approached him. "You're Plumb! You were shot down!" the man exclaimed. Caught off guard and shocked, Col. Plumb verified that he was correct and asked the man how he knew.

The stranger shared that he packed his parachute. Plumb gasped in surprise and gratitude. The man shook his hand and said, "I guess it worked."

Col. Plumb couldn't sleep that night. He kept thinking about all the hours the man spent at a long wooden table inside the ship folding the silks of each chute, holding in his hands the fate of someone he didn't even know.

He later became a nationally known speaker and, in an attempt to remind people of the importance of gratitude, he asks his audiences, "Who packed or is packing your parachute?"

He emphasizes that we should be grateful for people who, not only pack our physical parachute, but those who pack our emotional and spiritual parachute.

Begin Your *Gratitude* Action Plan Today.

One of the earliest children's programs on television is *Captain Kangaroo*. A rather corny character on the show went by the name Mr. Green Jeans. He reminded kids to say these magic words every day, "*Please* and *thank you.*" Sounds simple but it begins with us 'older kids'.

Keep a Gratitude Journal on your phone or paper and prayerfully record one person or thing each day that happens for which or whom you are grateful. *Make a commitment to look for opportunities to show or share gratitude* to at least one person daily by simply saying, "Thank you!"

The Red Car Theory

If you were asked how many red cars you saw yesterday, it's doubtful you could recall. But if you were told to count all the red cars you see tomorrow, you would be amazed at the number.

Of course, the difference is you're looking for them. It's the same with opportunities to show gratitude and kindness. If you look for them, it will astound you how many chances you have to share.

We are familiar with the saying, "I complained about my shoes until I saw a man who had no feet." When we feel disappointed or discouraged, it's a good practice to do what we learned in elementary school: stop, look, and listen to those around us.

Be the one leper who returned to thank Jesus for what He did. When we pause, observe, and then serve, we will become clearly aware of how blessed we are and will feel the urgency to thank God for Who He is and what He has done in our life!

Positive Points to Ponder

- Gratitude Reciprocates: Scientific research proves you will have more hope and optimism when you daily show gratitude to God and others.
- Feeling grateful but not expressing it is like wrapping a present and not giving it to anyone. Share gratitude today in every way!

3

If You Are Able — Come to the Table

As much as I enjoy good food, I cherish the time and conversations around a table with people even more.

As a speaker and trainer, for several years I traveled around the country and quickly learned that regardless of how delicious the meal is, eating alone is not fun.

When family or friends visit our home, even though there is plenty of space to sit in our living room or family room, many times we eventually end up talking at or near a dining table.

No figure in the Bible is more closely associated with meals than its central character, Jesus. He valued sharing a meal with others so much there are over fifteen occasions recorded in the gospels, including ten times in the gospel of Luke.

In his book, *A Meal With Jesus*, author Tim Chester shares, "In Luke's gospel Jesus is either going to a meal, at a meal, or coming from a meal."

Jesus enjoyed spending time at the table in people's homes with family, friends, followers, and even the Pharisees–religious leaders who constantly disagreed with Him.

He was criticized for eating and drinking with the 'wrong kind of people'—tax collectors and sinners, non-believers, the marginalized, the oppressed, poor and needy, the sick and outcasts. Matthew, a former despised tax collector who became a follower, records Jesus' response when asked why He did this.

Jesus shared that John the Baptizer didn't eat and drink with them and they criticized him. Then He reminded the group He *does* eat and drink with them and they call Him a glutton and a drunkard. Basically, 'make up your mind'.

The story of Jesus inviting Matthew to follow Him is an example of what His ministry was really about.

Snapshot Picture of Scripture (Matthew 9:9-13)

Jesus saw Matthew collecting taxes at his booth and called him to become one of His followers. Matthew immediately stood up, closed the door, and followed Christ.

Later Jesus and His disciples were enjoying a meal at Matthew's house, and a bunch of his tax collector buddies and other disreputable people joined them for some good food, fun, and fellowship.

The Pharisees couldn't believe Jesus, a Jewish rabbi, would associate with these kinds of people, so they asked the disciples why He ate with such scum and misfits.

Jesus overheard their question, and His response was a 'flashback burning bush moment'. It was so profound they just stood there in silence and had no idea what to say.

He told them 'healthy people don't need a doctor—sick people do'. And then reminded these phony pharisees that He 'didn't come to call those who *think* they are saints but people who *know* they are sinners'.

To state that tax collectors were hated by the Jews is an understatement. They not only collaborated with the Roman government, but they cheated their Jewish friends and family members.

After collecting the required money for taxes, they could charge any amount over that amount and put it in their own pockets. Not exactly a way to win friends and be recognized by the Jerusalem Better Business Bureau as Man of the Year.

So, when Jesus asked Matthew to follow Him and then accepted Matthew's invitation to wine and dine with him and his sinner friends, it was more than the Pharisees could handle. They wondered how He could lower Himself to mix and mingle with such unacceptable, low-life people of their society.

The phrase *tax collectors and sinners* is seen numerous times in the gospels. One reason is that the Pharisees considered anyone who did not keep all the hundreds of oral laws they added to the original Mosaic laws of the Old Testament to be a sinner.

Focus on the fellowship more than the food.

Of all the meals Jesus shared at a table with others, the Last Supper was one of the most significant moments in His entire ministry. Holy Communion has been a central act of worship for Christians during the last two thousand years.

It is a time to remember the ultimate sacrifice Christ made for us. It is a time to reflect on our relationship *with* Him and renew our commitment *to* Him. Many believers refer to this special time and place as the 'Lord's Table'.

Whether a meal was in the Upper Room or at someone's home, the central gathering place where Jesus usually enjoyed meals and the fellowship was at a table.

There is something special about gathering around a table to enjoy a meal. It brings us out of our own world and helps us bond with and focus on others.

The table our family gathered around growing up was given to us by a friend when I was about ten years old. It was stored in an old vacant house, and I remember loading it on a borrowed truck and taking it home. Years later, my parents gave it to Lucy and me and we still use it every day.

If that 75-year-old table could talk, it would share some of the most memorable times, experiences, and conversations of our family.

Memories of laughing around the table as we celebrated special holiday meals, birthdays, graduations, and Jon and Chris eating breakfast while watching ESPN highlights. And serious conversations about jobs or college and evening meals after a long day at school or work.

That special table was and is so much more than a piece of furniture. Pause and reflect on memories you have of meaningful conversations around a table.

Life Changing Lessons At the Table:

Eating together at a table connects us. It helps us overcome any barriers that might separate us. It's an incredible way to share feelings and fellowship with others. The table might be at a fine dining restaurant, a home-cooked meal, a latte at a coffee shop, or sharing a banana split with two spoons.

The type of table is irrelevant. It could be spending time together around a kitchen table, picnic table, card table, or restaurant table. It's all about fellowship and relationships.

Make a memory today by inviting someone to join you around a table. Call or text a friend or family member with whom you haven't spent time with lately.

Jesus met people and connected with them where they were and expects us to do the same. He called the disciples when they were cleaning their nets and talked about fishing. He called Matthew when he was collecting money.

I believe if He was in the rural area where we live, He would climb up in the back of someone's pickup truck on a farm and start teaching them how to plant seeds in people's hearts.

Jesus was often criticized for socializing and enjoying meals with the wrong kind of people. He made it clear that everyone was welcome at His table. It is awesome that He still welcomes, loves, and accepts everyone around His table–including you and me!

Positive Points to Ponder
- My family and friends may not have it all together but when we're together, it feels like we have it all.
- Gather around the table–where stories are told, laughter is bold, and sweet memories are created to hold.

4

Too Blessed to Be Stressed

Lucy and I had been married a few years when we decided to make the eight-hour road trip from Virginia to visit the big city. Not just any big city. *The* big city–New York. Where the yellow cabs roam and the traffic is nothing like back home.

We are both from the small town of Blacksburg. So, the bumper-to-bumper traffic with thousands of drivers honking their horns two minutes *before* the lights turn green created a highly stressful experience.

This was decades before GPS was available. I tried listening to Lucy as she shared driving instructions from the Rand McNally Road Atlas map to navigate our way to the Statue of Liberty.

Attempting to locate specific streets without hitting one of the hundreds of crossing pedestrians—even though the big red hand was displayed—created more anxiety than I could handle.

At my ultimate level of stress, I grabbed the map from Lucy, used both hands to crumple it into a little ball, rolled down the window, and threw it onto the street!

Of course, Lucy, always cool and collected, looked at me and calmly asked the classic question, "Well, *now* what are we going to do? Not only do we not know how to get there, we don't even know where we are." For one of the few times in my life, I had nothing to say.

In the gospel of Luke, we find the story of a stressful situation involving an argument between two sisters. Imagine that—a disagreement between family members.

Snapshot Picture of Scripture (Luke 10:38-42)

Jesus and his disciples were visiting the home of two sisters, Mary and Martha. They were the sisters of Lazarus, and all were close friends with Jesus. While Mary was spending time with Jesus, Martha was busy cleaning the house and preparing a meal.

Martha wasn't getting any help from Mary and in her frustration complained to Jesus. She actually asked Him if He cared that she was doing all the work by herself and to tell Mary to help her. Does that sound familiar?

Jesus told Martha she shouldn't worry and get upset over things that are temporary. Then He basically shared that Mary had made the right choice by spending time with Him and making relationships a priority.

Martha, Martha, Martha…

I can picture Martha, who after cleaning the house by herself and working over a hot stove in the kitchen, finally thinks, "This is not fair. Enough is enough." Stressed out and with flour covering her apron, she hurriedly leaves the bread baking and the soup boiling, rushes out of the kitchen, and rudely interrupts Jesus.

(It reminds me of a familiar story about a guy who stressed out and lost his cool while trying to drive around New York City.)

I can visualize Jesus sitting and chatting with Mary and when Martha interrupted, He understood why.

Jesus smiles, looks at Martha and calmly responds, "Martha, Martha, Martha. Just take a breath and chill out. What you're doing is a good thing. But Mary has her priorities right and has chosen to stop and take advantage of listening to me and learn what I am teaching."

There is a story of a farmer who lost his watch in an old barn. He looked everywhere with no success and since it had sentimental value, he asked some kids playing outside to help him find it.

After about 30 minutes one little boy came running out with the watch. When the farmer asked how he found it, the boy replied that he sat down in silence and listened. When he heard the ticking sound, he followed it to the watch.

Like Mary, sometimes we need to sit and listen as Jesus leads and guides us. A reminder that when we rearrange the letters in the word SILENT, we have the word LISTEN. (Psalm 46:10)

Jesus loved Martha. It wasn't wrong that she wanted to take care of her to-do list. It was just the wrong timing. When God calls us to sit at His feet, we need to drop what we are doing, draw near to Him and enjoy His presence.

Author Joanne Liggan shares in her book, *FACTS: Faith And Commitment Through Scripture,* how all of Martha's worrying about preparations was not as important as what Mary was doing. Time spent with the Lord is more important than anything else you can do.

And time enjoying His presence and blessings should not be taken for granted. *In a society that has you counting money, pounds, calories, and steps, slow down and take time to count your blessings!*

Triggers and Triumphs of Worry and Stress

The first trigger of stress is *perspective*—how you see life's challenges. Have you ever noticed how some people get upset over the smallest problem while others keep their cool no matter what happens? It all depends on how they view the situation in their mind.

Some view every daily challenge they encounter as physically or emotionally threatening. Since they have no perspective, most situations will seem to be a major problem for them.

While others visualize challenges with a proper perspective. They understand there are some situations of which they have no control and therefore, there is no reason to be anxious.

The title of the book by Richard Carlson says it best: *Don't Sweat the Small Stuff and It's All Small Stuff.*

The second trigger of stress is *worry*.

4 Reasons Not to Worry:

In his book, *The Purpose Driven Life*, author and pastor Rick Warren shares four important reminders why Christians shouldn't worry:

1. *Worry Is Unreasonable:* To worry about something you can't change is useless.
2. *Worry Is Unnatural:* We weren't born a worrier. It's a learned response.
3. *Worry Is Unhelpful:* Worrying about a problem never solves the problem.
4. *Worry Is Unnecessary:* God has promised to take care of you, so trust Him.

In the Sermon on the Mount, Jesus shared some profound thoughts about worrying.

"That is why I tell you not to worry about everyday life–whether you have enough food and drink, or enough clothes to wear. Isn't life more important than food, and your body more than clothing? Can all your worries add a single moment to your life? So don't worry about tomorrow, for tomorrow will bring its own worries. Today's trouble is enough for today" (Matthew 6:25, 27, 34 NLT).

Everyone needs a good worry-washing.

The story is told of a crowd standing under the awning outside a store waiting for a gutter-washing rain to stop. A little girl was heard asking her mom if they could run through the rain, to which her mom told her they couldn't make it through the downpour and needed to wait until it let up.

The little girl persisted and said, "That's not what you said this morning. Don't you remember? When we were talking to daddy about his cancer you said, 'If God can help us make it through this, He can get us through anything.'"

The entire crowd stopped talking. Dead silence. You could hear nothing but the rain. No one came or left. Then the mother's words broke the silence as she pulled up her raincoat hood and said, "Honey, you're exactly right. If God lets us get wet, well maybe we just need a good worry-washing."

Everyone watched as they ran, laughed, and splashed through puddles. And then one by one everyone eventually ran—and got wet. That little girl reminds us, as Mary demonstrated, relationships and spending time with others should always be our top priority.

How to Stifle Stress
- *Unlike Martha (and me), keep situations in perspective.* When feeling stressed use the *555 Rule*. Ask yourself if the problem you're stressed about will still matter 5 days, 5 months, or 5 years from now. There will be events and situations that will matter the rest of your life. But most of our worries never happen or aren't nearly as negative as we thought.
- *Like Mary, choose priorities and keep the main thing the main thing.* Your to-do list is never as important as other people.
LOVE is spelled T-I-M-E.
- *Remember Jesus shared that worrying can't add another hour to your life.* In 1 Peter he gives us some valuable advice regarding what to do and the reason when he tells us to 'give all our worries and cares to God because He cares about you.'

Positive Points to Ponder

- You are truly blessed:
  Your terrible job is the dream of the unemployed.
  Your mediocre house is the dream of the homeless.
  Your smile is the dream of the depressed.
  Your health is the dream of the seriously ill.
  Don't let your difficult times make you forget your blessings!

- *Trust*–in His timing
  Rely–on His promises
  Wait–on His answers
  Believe–in His miracles
  Rejoice–in His goodness
  Relax– in His presence

5

Mistakes and Mess-Ups Make You a Masterpiece

During a recent conversation with friends, someone casually asked the group, "If you could correct one mistake or decision from the past, what would it be?"

My personal Mistakes and Mess-Ups Memo would be a rather lengthy list but would definitely include how I failed to apply myself academically during high school.

Someone attempted to state the situation positively as, 'I was in the half of my graduating class that made the upper half possible'. Admittedly, I didn't take studying and making top grades seriously until my later years in education.

My report cards usually contained more than one teacher commenting, *Jerry is not working up to his potential*. It would have benefited me greatly had I spent more time on subjects like social studies and less on socializing.

It took a wakeup conversation with a teacher who shared her belief that I have unlimited God-given potential and my 'gift of gab' could be used to positively impact the lives of others.

In hindsight I believe that my big mess-up and a tendency to enjoy talking was a motivating factor to inspire others later in life as a teacher, counselor, pastor, speaker, and trainer.

In scripture we can find numerous examples of how our mistakes don't have to define us or be the end of our life-story.

Snapshot Picture of Scripture (John 4:4-42)

The story of the Samaritan woman begins with Jesus being in the small village of Sychar. Jews rarely passed through this area, as Samaritans were considered social outcasts and hated by both Gentiles and Jews.

Around noon, the hottest part of the day when most people were resting, Jesus sat at a popular well. A Samaritan woman came to draw water, so Jesus asked her for a drink.

When she asked why a Jew would ask a Samaritan for water, He told her He had something better—*Living Water*—and added that she would never be thirsty again.

Then Jesus asked her to go get her husband, to which she admitted she didn't have one. Jesus agreed and then shocked her by sharing that He knew she previously had five husbands and wasn't married to the man with whom she was now living.

The truth hurt, but she was amazed and excited that she had found the Messiah everyone was waiting for. She left her water vase at the well, rushed into town, and told everyone about a man she met who told her everything she had done in her life.

Because of her bad reputation not everyone believed her. But her testimony convinced many Samaritans to follow her to hear Jesus, and they too became believers.

Christ used this disrespected woman with a terrible reputation to spread the Good News in spite of the fact that she had made way too many mistakes in her life.

In first century Jewish culture, women were treated as second-class citizens with few of the rights had by men. But Jesus crossed those barriers and treated all people with equal respect and love.

Your value doesn't depend on your past.

What would it be like to meet someone who told you all the mistakes or sins you committed during your life? The first thing I would do is look around to make sure no one else was listening. For most of us it would not be an enjoyable experience and likely very embarrassing.

One of the most unique characteristics of the Bible, compared to books of other beliefs, is that it doesn't cover up the mess-ups and mistakes of the leaders of our Christian faith. It contains the good, bad, and the ugly of some of the most well-known and respected leaders.

Author Jim Daly offers several examples: Noah got drunk, Jacob lied, Moses was a murderer, Gideon was afraid, Rahab was a prostitute, David was an adulterer, Elijah was suicidal, Isaiah preached naked, Jonah ran from God, Job went bankrupt, Peter denied Christ, the disciples were weak and jealous, Martha was anxious and worried about everything, Mary Magdalene was demon possessed, and the apostle Paul was a terrorist who hunted down Christians! *If you have made mistakes and messed up, you're in good company!*

What these people did was not the end of their story. They allowed God to change their *hearts,* and He used them to change their *world.* **Don't let the enemy steal your story—let Christ rewrite it!**

I facilitated a seminar and held up a twenty-dollar bill for the audience to see. When I asked for a show of hands verifying who wanted it, almost every hand went up. Then I crumpled it up in a ball, asked the same question and most hands went up again. I threw it on the floor and stomped on it several times, followed by the same question, and received an identical response.

I shared that as we travel through life everyone makes mistakes, or is mistreated, disrespected, or possibly abused. But that doesn't make us any less valuable as a person. *We are still a masterpiece in God's eyes.*

Know who you really are. Most people have a tendency to settle for so much less than what God intended. Because they've made mistakes or people have treated them wrongly, they value themselves as 'on sale or a clearance special'. **Don't ever let someone's opinion of you or what you've done become your final reality.**

I once heard someone say, "I've discovered the enemy. It's me." Are you your enemy? Are you limiting your dreams or a relationship because you don't feel valuable? Remember your value to God is beyond your imagination. No matter what you've done, He loves you.

David gives us a glimpse in Psalms when he shares that we are more valuable than all the grains of sand. Pause and think about that statement.

There are five hundred million grains of sand in one cubic foot. Consider how many grains there might be on all the beaches in the world. Add all the sand under all the oceans. Now add all the grains of sand in all the deserts. Well, you get the point. You are more valuable than you can comprehend.

Your worth is not a result of *who* you are but *whose* you are. Regardless of your mistakes, mess-ups, unwise decisions, or sin, don't ever doubt your value to God.

When you feel inadequate, unworthy, or unloved, remember you are a son or daughter of our Heavenly Father. He will forgive you and can do great things through you! God will never separate Himself from you and will always love you!

In Romans we find that 'nothing in the sky above, or in the earth, and nothing in all creation will ever be able to separate us from the love of God'.

Turning A Mess Into A Masterpiece
Yes, I'm a Christian.
Yes, I still make mistakes.
Yes, I still struggle.
Yes, I still fail.
Yes, I still can be a mess.
But, I'm now God's mess.
And God can turn a mess
into a masterpiece!

Positive Points to Ponder
- Sometimes God has a funny way of doing things. For example, He'll pick up a nobody and turn them into somebody in front of everybody without asking anybody.

- God didn't add another day to your life because *you* needed it. He added it because you are valuable, and someone needs you—*today*!

6

The Power of Purpose and Passion

For years our family has stood with thousands of Virginia Tech Hokie football fans in jam-packed, sold-out Lane Stadium. As the team runs out of the tunnel onto the field, *Enter Sandman* blasts over the PA system and the crowd erupts in a thunderous roar.

With fireworks exploding in the sky, everyone starts jumping with so much energy it feels like the stadium is literally shaking. ESPN once selected Lane Stadium as one of the best game entrances and one of the top ten best environments in which to watch a college football game.

The passion we have for our team is obvious. And the purpose that creates the passion is our desire to support and encourage the players to compete at their highest level to win.

When we discover our purposes in life it creates a higher level of passion for living. This simple truth is illustrated in the conversion story of the apostle Paul.

Snapshot Picture of Scripture (Acts 9:3-19)
Before Paul became a follower of Christ, he intensely persecuted Christians and participated in the killing of Stephen, the first martyr for Christ.

One day he was on his way to Damascus with the intention of arresting men and women who were followers of Jesus and bringing them to Jerusalem in chains.

But his journey was interrupted when suddenly an extremely bright light flashed around him. He immediately fell to the ground and heard the voice of the resurrected Christ ask why he was persecuting Him.

When he got up he couldn't see, and following Jesus' instructions was led by the shocked witnesses who were with him to Damascus. He was completely blind while staying there for three days. Ananias, a follower of Christ, prayed with him, and he miraculously regained his sight.

Since he was born into a Jewish family who also had Roman citizenship, he had a dual name, Saul (Hebrew) and Paul (Roman). After his conversion he wanted to minister to all people, not just the Jews, and eventually was known as Paul. He became one of the most impactful leaders of the Christian faith.

After he found God's true purpose for his life, Paul became so passionate for the cause of Christ it's mind-boggling the positive impact he made for Jesus.

As a missionary he is credited with starting at least 20 churches, and scholars credit him with writing at least 13 of the 27 books in the New Testament!

Finding Purpose and Passion.

According to a recent research poll, only 20% of workers in America are passionate about their jobs. One main reason given is some people don't see a real purpose in what they do.

There are three basic questions most people want answered: Why am I here? Am I making a difference? What is my purpose in life?

Rick Warren shares *five important principles of purpose and passion*.
1. We were *planned* for God's purpose.
   Love Him and offer real worship.
2. We were *formed* for God's purpose.
   Enjoy real fellowship with others.
3. We were *created* to become like Christ.
   Learn real discipleship.
4. We were *shaped* to serve God.
   Practice real ministry right where you are.
   (You don't have to be a pastor or missionary

to show and share God's love.)
5. We were *made* for a mission.
Use your unique God-given talents for His purposes.

As you seek God's purposes, keep in mind there is life beyond this one. Earth isn't your final destination. You are just a tourist passing through. Since we are only here a short time, it is important that we find and live God's purpose for our lives.

Passion and Purpose Go Together. Some things become better when combined: peanut butter and jelly, burger and fries, spaghetti and meatballs, and macaroni and cheese.

When we discover our unique purpose, we will become passionate. It will be obvious as purpose and passion go together to potentially form a life-changing combination.

Ask anyone who believes their vocation is a *calling* and you will see a high level of passion and enthusiasm. A passion for Christ honors Him, gives us peace, and influences others.

Paul shares, "... your enthusiasm has stirred most of them to action" (2 Corinthians 9:2 NIV).

You may not have a light-blinding experience like Paul when you find your unique purpose. For most people it's a gradual process that is felt and grows in their heart.

Remember you are uniquely made in the image of God for His purposes that you can help fulfill.

"Many are the plans in the mind of a man, but it is the purpose of the LORD that will stand" (Proverbs 19:21 ESV).

Think of it like this. Hold up your hand and visualize a glove beside it. A glove is made in the image of a hand. Without the hand a glove has no purpose. But because it was formed in the image of the hand, when the hand gets inside the glove it then has purpose.

You were made in the image of God and when you become a believer, His Spirit is inside you and you can discover His purpose for your life.

Mary Clark, a mother in LA, lost her son and decided to donate his heart. The recipient was a twelve-year-old boy dying of a heart disease.

She eventually visited the boy, and after hugs and tears were shared, was handed a stethoscope. She placed it on his chest and listened to the heartbeat of her son who had passed away, now inside this little boy.

Pause and let that last thought marinate a moment. Can you imagine the emotion of hearing your child's heartbeat inside another child—giving him a new life? A new life with a new purpose and passion.

God is not just the starting point of your life; He is the source of it. Living on purpose—with His purpose—is the only way to really live.

Positive Points to Ponder
- No matter what people may think, God made you for a reason and purpose. You are an original, and an original is always worth more than a copy.
- Your story is important. Your dreams count. Your voice matters. You were born to make an impact. Your life has purpose!

7

Now Get A REAL Life

Several years ago I wrote a book titled *Now Get A Real Life: How to Create the Fulfilling Life You Were Born to Live*. It was based on the verse found in *The Message* translation that Jesus 'came so that we could have a *real* life, more and better than we could ever dream of'.

Some translations of John 10:10b use the word abundantly. The word *abundantly* is one of the most misinterpreted words in this passage. Sometimes a little exaggerated humor and sharing what a word does not mean actually helps clarify its true definition.

Enjoy the words of the song by recording artist Ray Stevens, "Would Jesus Wear A Rolex?". He describes watching someone on television who obviously missed what Jesus meant when He used the word *abundance*.

> "He wore designer clothes, and a big smile on his face,
> Sellin' me salvation while they sang Amazing Grace;
> Askin' me for money, he had all the signs of wealth,
> I almost wrote a check out, but then I caught myself.
>
> Would Jesus wear a pinky ring, would He drive a fancy car?
> Would His wife wear furs and diamonds, would His dressing room have a star?
> If He came back tomorrow, well there's something I'd like to know;
> Would Jesus wear a Rolex on His television show?"

To clarify, God definitely chooses to bless many believers financially—including ministers. Let's look at the context of this verse in which Jesus is teaching about the abundant life or a life that is real and full.

Snapshot Picture of Scripture (John 10:7-18)

In the first part of John 10, Jesus tells the Pharisees a parable emphasizing that He is the gatekeeper of the sheep pen. His sheep will recognize His voice and follow Him.

But the Pharisees didn't have a clue as to what He was telling them, so hoping their mental light bulb would turn on, He shared another parable.

In the second story He explains that He is the Good Shepherd who loves His sheep so much He is willing to lay down His life for them and give them a life of abundance.

What abundance is *not*.

As someone once shared, "Let me make one thing perfectly clear." When Jesus describes a life with Him as abundant, it had absolutely nothing to do with accumulating material possessions.

The Bible consistently tells us that wealth, prestige, position, and power *in this world* are not His priorities for us. Physical blessings may or may not be part of a God-centered life. Neither our wealth nor our poverty is a sure indication of our standing with God.

Once they became followers none of Jesus' disciples were wealthy or lived a lavish lifestyle. Luke shares in Chapter 6 that when Jesus sent them on a mission trip, He told them not to take anything with them. Don't take food, money, a change of clothes, or a traveler's bag. And He instructed them to stay in people's homes.

If His message was about the importance of getting more 'stuff', then Jesus himself would have been one of the richest men on earth. Instead, He depended on family, friends, followers, and His Heavenly Father for food and shelter and was homeless during most of His ministry.

Many people sincerely seeking spiritual truth have been deceived by leaders of the prosperity gospel or the theology also known as the health and wealth gospel or the seed-of-faith movement.

These folk believe through positive confession they have a divine right to prosper in all areas of their life, especially finances.

It emphasizes that faith, expressed through declarations and donations, draws an abundance of health, wealth, and happiness into believers' lives.

But the true meaning of abundance far exceeds financial or health well-being in this life.

What Jesus means by abundance.

In Greek, *abundant* means beyond measure or exceedingly. In describing the abundant life found in this passage, various scripture translations offer the words; full, fulfilling, eternal, or real.

Think of it as Jesus promising us a life that's better than we could ever imagine. As Paul shares, "Now to Him who by the power at work within us is able to accomplish abundantly far more than we can ask or imagine" (Ephesians 3:20 NRSV).

If we seek an abundant life through Christ, we can find a life that is abundant in things that are eternal and not temporary. Abundant in real love, abundant in real joy, abundant in real peace, abundant in real forgiveness and grace.

Begin living a real, abundant life now.

Real is a root word for reality. Reality television shows exploded in the early 2000's. Interestingly, a recent survey gives results that most viewers admit there is very little about a reality show that resembles real life.

Scientists share that we need four things to survive in this life: water, air, food, and light. Scripture tells us Christ is:

> The Living Water–John 4:10
> The Breath of Life–Job 33:4
> The Bread of Life–John 6:35
> The Light of the World–John 8:1-2

God doesn't want you to wait until you leave this world and are checking in at heaven's front desk getting your new house key to begin living a truly abundant life. He wants to affect your life right now!

Jesus describes Himself in this second parable of John 10 as the Good Shepherd. He stores up goodness for us. There is never a shortage of goodness—there is plenty for everyone at His table.

As much as I enjoy eating desserts, if I ate them at every meal every day, my level of enjoyment would decrease.

Similarly, if we were showered with nothing but God's abundant goodness 24/7, we probably wouldn't recognize or appreciate it. He may store it and make sure we receive it when we need it. He gave the Israelites in the wilderness just enough manna for each day. So, don't hesitate to ask.

He desires to give you a life in Him that is meaningful, purposeful, joyful, and eternal, overflowing abundantly with joy, peace, and His love!

Positive Points to Ponder
- This season in your life can be used to prepare you for a life of God's goodness and eternal abundance.
- Allow God to give you a life of true abundance and pray for the ability to:
    Suffer with a smile
    Praise in the pain
    Worship instead of worry
    Get ready for greater *abundance*!

8

Broken and Restored Makes Us Better Than Before

Gary, a good friend of mine for years, has been in the car business most of his life. One of the businesses he owns, Duncan Imports and Classic Cars, is also used to share the Good News of Christ.

He provides a conference room at the facility for our weekly men's Bible Study group—which we call 'Tuesday Morning Church'. Jerry, (another Jerry), is our faithful leader, and I'm blessed to be a part of such an incredibly dedicated group of guys.

In addition to a place for greeting customers, the entrance to the facility is also used to make complimentary Bibles, Christian books, and other resources available to visitors.

He shared an interesting story with me about his very first car. Before he was even old enough to have a driver's license, he and another guy purchased an old run-down 1957 Thunderbird. To say it was in rough shape is an understatement.

The original paint was blue but had turned an ugly black. The engine would barely run, and the interior was faded and worn. Gary and his buddy overhauled the engine, replaced the interior, and painted the car its original beautiful blue. It was more in demand than when it was new because it was *broken and restored and looked better than before.*

Sometimes relationships need to be restored. A disagreement between the apostle Paul and one of his missionary colleagues created a situation of much-needed restoration.

Snapshot Picture of Scripture (Acts 15:36-39a and 2 Timothy 4:11)

During the apostle Paul's missionary journeys, he needed the assistance of a number of helpers. But sometimes the help he received was less than agreeable.

Barnabas wanted to take John Mark with him, but Paul didn't think it wise to take him because he had deserted them earlier. They had such a strong disagreement they parted ways, which broke their relationship.

We don't hear any more about Mark or Barnabas for the remainder of Acts. Thankfully, we eventually get to see how the story ends. After Paul was put in prison near the end of his life, he reunited with Mark and *restored their broken relationship*.

Broken for a reason and only for a season.

Unbroken, a book by Lauren Hillenbrand, is the amazing true story of Louis Zamperini who gains national attention for competing in the 1936 Berlin Olympics.

During World War II his military plane is shot down and he miraculously survives many challenges including a long sea journey on a raft and then years of cruel treatment as a prisoner of war.

After returning home he struggles with his war demons and alcohol abuse. His marriage and life were broken. The story ends with a miraculous reconciliation with God and the restoration of his relationship with his wife.

Broken Areas in Life That Can Be Restored

Relationships. Broken or strained relationships are not always, but usually worth trying to restore. If you're struggling in this area, remember to focus on the relationship and not the resolution. Most importantly, your relationship with your Heavenly Father.

"God blesses those who work for peace, for they will be called the children of God" (Matthew 5:9 NLT).

Finances. Job was a very wealthy man who lost everything he owned and his entire family. But as a result of his faithfulness, the Lord eventually allowed his fortunes to be restored.

Physical or Emotional Health. Because of her faith a woman who had been bleeding for twelve years was healed by Jesus. Faith is necessary for restoring all brokenness.

Scripture tells us that Jesus turned around, and when He saw her said, "Daughter, be encouraged! Your faith has made you well" (Matthew 9:22 NLT).

Lost the Joy of Living. Even during tough times our joy can be restored. David was literally running for his life, filled with anxiety, when he stopped and prayed for God to restore his joy.

Being broken can turn out to be a good thing.

The Japanese have a long history of repairing ceramic pottery using the art of *Kintsugi*, which means *golden joinery*.

When someone cracks or chips their favorite vessel or teacup, it is not thrown away. Instead, a craftsman fills the broken or cracked areas with a gold resin powder.

The art of *Kintsugi* is the ability to see value in brokenness, and many people actually value the once-broken pottery more *after* it has been restored.

Do you sometimes feel broken? If so, the same lessons learned from the art of *Kintsugi* apply to your relationship with God. After He restores:

- You are more beautiful.
- You are more valuable.
- You are stronger.
- You have a unique story to share.
- You are a new creation.

Some of the brokenness you have experienced was not to show or prove anything to others. It was to show these truths to you so you will be able to say, "With God's help this isn't going to break me."

And during those times when you do feel broken, God has the ability to restore you and put you back together. So, you are more beautiful, more valuable, stronger, have a new story to share, and most importantly, are a new creation in Him!

Positive Points to Ponder
- God uses broken people. It takes broken soil to produce a crop, broken clouds to give us rain, and broken bread to give us strength.
- God can mend your broken heart today if you will give Him all the broken pieces. The God who made you can also mend you!

9

Magic, Myth or Miracle?

When our sons Jon and Chris were in elementary school, Lucy and I changed jobs and decided to move to the small, quaint town of Floyd—about 30 miles away.

After unsuccessfully driving up and down the streets—all four of them—looking for For Sale signs in yards, I finally chose a house at random, parked in the driveway, and knocked on the front door.

I asked the kind lady who came to the door if she was aware of any houses in town that were for sale. She paused, and then to my surprise shared that it hadn't been advertised, but actually she was planning to sell her house!

After several conversations and only four weeks later, we were in our attorney's office closing the sale!

Has something similar ever happened to you? Something you knew was more than a coincidence, yet unexplainable? Possibly some kind of a magical blessing, or maybe this miracle thing wasn't a myth.

As we discover some exciting insights about miracles and how they relate to our lives, let's look at one recorded in the gospel of John. He records seven 'signs and wonders' that point to Christ as the Messiah.

Snapshot Picture of Scripture (John 5:1-9a)

This story takes place during one of three annual Jewish festivals in Jerusalem at a pool near the Sheep Gate—where livestock are brought to the temple to be sacrificed.

As Jesus enters the pool area, He sees five covered porches packed with sick people who are afflicted, paralyzed or blind, and feeling helpless and hopeless.

He looked around and focused on a man who had been laying there for 38 years. Jesus stepped over and around ailing people, approached the man, and asked him if he wanted to get well. At the time it seemed like a strange question. What lame person wouldn't want to be healed?

The man, unaware of who Jesus was, believed he could be healed only if he could get in the pool when the water bubbles up. He responded to Jesus' question that he needed someone to carry him to the pool.

Jesus told him to stand up, pick up his mat, and walk. In faith the man was immediately healed. He stood, picked up his mat, and started walking!

Can you imagine the reaction of not only the healed man, but all the other sick people who were watching this miracle? They had known this man to lay near the pool unable to move for 38 years. And now they are watching him carry his mat through the crowds!

It is interesting that out of all the people, Jesus chose this man. He didn't walk to the pool area and yell, "Excuse me, could I please have your attention for just a moment? Everyone who would like to be healed please raise your hand. Raise them high so I can see them."

He focused on this one man and personally asked if he wanted to be well—possibly so the man would acknowledge his need and to test his faith.

I can visualize in my own mind Jesus possibly turning to His followers with Him, winking and quietly whispering something like, "Hold my coffee and watch this." Not 'watch *me*'. But telling them to 'watch these people's reaction when they see what My Heavenly Father does through Me'.

Just like the paralyzed man, Jesus cares about each of us. When He tells us to do something and we trust, believe, and obey, our lives can dramatically change.

Miracles...

In our culture the word *miracle* is often used to describe different situations:

"It's a miracle we won the game." "We call her our miracle baby." "They say it's a miracle drug and works wonders." "He was diagnosed with a terminal disease, but because of a miracle it disappeared."

Let's consider the definitions of miracle.
1. An event that appears inexplicable by the laws of nature and so is held to be supernatural or an act of God; divine intervention; signs and wonders.

2. An amazing, outstanding, surprising, unexpected event or series of events

Some people have a problem believing in miracles. Our puny natural minds have difficulty understanding the supernatural and don't realize, or aren't willing to admit, it's a God-thing.

Others wonder if God still works miracles today. Apologist and author of *The Case for Miracles: A Journalist Investigates Evidence for the Supernatural*, Lee Strobel, shares, "Not only is the miraculous still possible, but God still intervenes in our world in awe-inspiring ways."

And there's the question of some regarding why doesn't God heal everyone? (By the way, it's *not* because they lack faith.) In this passage Jesus apparently walked around all the other diseased folk at the pool, as John only records Him healing one man.

Sometimes God's blessings come in other ways than physical healing. If good health were always God's will, then Christians should never die.

Nick Vuijick was born without arms or legs and now leads a ministry program, *Life Without Limbs*, which has reached millions with the Good News of Christ.

When asked why he hasn't been healed, Nick responded, "I pray for the miracle of getting arms and legs and have a pair of shoes in my closet—just in case God says yes to me. I believe *when you don't get a miracle you can be a miracle for someone else.*"

For believers everything happens for a reason.

We sometimes forget that we serve a BIG God. He is omnipotent (in total control of everything), omniscient (knows everything), and omnipresent (everywhere all the time).

When believers understand that everything happens for a reason, and nothing happens by chance, they are acknowledging the fact that God is aware and a part of every situation in our lives. Not just the big events, but the small stuff of daily living. Events and situations are not just a coincidence.

The author of *When God Winks*, Squire Rushnell, shares, "Sometimes coincidences are the best way for God to establish a perpetual presence in your life. What are the odds of some things happening? God speaks in different ways, some of which could be the miracle of a connection of events."

Don't miss his statement about the possibility of a connection of events that are not always quick and instantaneous. Miracles aren't always in a fast Jiffy-Pop or Drive-Through time frame.

Former college and professional football star Tim Tebow made a pregame habit of marking John 3:16 under his eyes as a witness for Christ. After a playoff game someone informed him of the following statistics for the game.

Total Passing yards–316
Average yards rushing–3.16
Average yards per catch–31.6
Time of possession–31.06

Reading these statistics a reporter approached him and said, "Big coincidence." Tim looked at him, smiled and replied, "Big God."

Be aware of daily miracles, beginning with the fact that God blessed you with another day to live. Whether you refer to them as divine interventions, God Winks, or miracles, if you seek you will find.

And when you are seeking and praying for a miracle in your life, remember the words of Jesus, "...with God all things are possible."

Positive Points to Ponder
- Remember, every miracle in the Bible started with a big problem. Tell God yours and then look for His answer.
- Most of us are looking for a burning bush or waiting for our ship to come in. Take the time to pray every day and look for the little road signs (miracles) that lead us in the direction to God.

10

Always on Time Every Time

I don't like to wait on anyone in any situation at any time. I'm the guy who, when approaching traffic lights, switches lanes to save three seconds. When choosing a checkout line at the store I've been known to count the customers in each line before making a commitment. And if the line I chose moves too slowly I will strongly consider changing lines again.

It's interesting that most medical facilities *expect* us to wait. In fact, they have a special area specifically for this purpose, designated as the *waiting room*.

It may surprise you how much time we spend waiting. According to a recent poll we wait thirty-eight hours a year at traffic lights, thirteen hours a year on hold, and five years of our life in line…waiting!

I found encouraging facts about some leading Bible characters: Abraham and Sarah waited 25 years for her to become pregnant, Joseph waited 22 years to reconcile with his brothers; Moses waited 40 years wandering in the desert; and Jesus waited 30 years to begin His ministry. It appears that we're all in good company if we have to wait.

The Biblical account of Noah is filled with life lessons of faith and a powerful example of the importance of waiting on God's timing.

Snapshot Picture of Scripture (Genesis 6-8)

Before the earth was destroyed by the Great Flood, God gave Noah an opportunity for he and his family to be saved. He received detailed instructions on how to build a big boat, the specific dimensions, and what to put in it.

Noah and his family built the ark and filled it with pairs of every kind of land animal on the earth at that time. Once the rain started it continued for forty days and forty nights.

When the water finally receded, it was time for Noah, his family and all the animals to leave the ark. One of the first things he did was build an altar and give thanks to the Lord.

God was pleased with Noah's obedience and sent a rainbow to establish a covenant and remind people the earth would never again be destroyed by flood.

The time Noah spent waiting: As he and his family worked on building the ark they *waited* on the flood for about 100 years. They *waited* for 40 days and nights for the rain to stop, then *waited* 150 more days for the water to recede.

I can't imagine waiting that long for anything. It's interesting that the dimensions of the ark—six times longer than its width—were used by modern shipbuilders for years. Noah's faith while waiting is further shown by the fact the ark didn't have a steering wheel. They just floated for about six months.

Our bad time can be God's glad time.

Waiting in line or traffic is one thing, but waiting for an extended period of time for an answered prayer is an entirely different situation.

I have to remind myself, one of the reasons we wait is the promises God has for us are usually discovered in the process. And the process will always require–you guessed it–waiting.

During the up and down seasons in our life that may appear as a *bad* time, could be the *very* time God will bless us.

He likes to bless people; when they just received a negative health report, when someone just walked out on them, when they just lost their job, when someone they loved passed away, or when someone said something that crushed them to their core.

Only God knows the time He will step in. A reference to waiting is mentioned in the Bible 116 times. He knows how difficult it is to wait. Believe the promises in His Word are true and He will be faithful to you.

"Be still before the LORD and wait patiently on Him" (Psalm 37:7 NIV). "For they who wait for the LORD shall renew their strength; they shall mount up with wings like eagles; they shall run and not be weary; they shall walk and not faint" (Isaiah 40:31 ESV).

God is working while we are waiting. We tend to think if we don't see immediate results, He isn't doing anything. But as soon as we pray, He puts in the order for shipping and starts working on it. We just don't know the date of arrival.

It's like planting a Chinese bamboo tree. It has to be watered and fertilized every day. Yet it doesn't break through the ground for five years. Five years of waiting. But once it breaks through it can miraculously grow up to 90 feet in five weeks!

It was growing for 5 years beneath the surface but was not visible.

Life lessons from Noah:
1. Don't miss the boat.
2. Remember we're all in the same boat.
3. Plan ahead. It wasn't raining when Noah started building the ark
4. Build your future on higher ground.
5. Remember the ark was built by amateurs; the Titanic by professionals.
6. No matter how severe the storms of life, when you are with God there is always a rainbow.
7. When you're stressed out while waiting–just float for a while.

The Hebrew definition of the word *wait* includes hope, anticipation, and trust in God. He is using these times of waiting to teach and train us for what lies ahead. The secret to peace with God is to discover, accept, and appreciate God's perfect timing.

"For everything there is a season, and a time for every purpose under heaven" (Ecc. 3:1 ASV).

God will answer your prayers. Until then, He promises it will be worth the wait. **He will always be on time, at the right time, every time!**

Positive Points to Ponder
- While you're waiting on God do what waiters do; serve.
- When we rush God's timing we make a mess. Trust his timing. True love always waits.

11

Pain Purifies Your Priorities

No Pain–No Gain is a commonly seen motto in many fitness facilities. The implication is if people want to improve their long-term health, they must be willing to experience some temporary pain. For years it was thought the longer someone works out and the more pain they endure while exercising, the better their level of fitness.

Interestingly, the same morning I started writing this chapter on pain, Lucy shared that she was having excruciating pain in her lower side. A few minutes later she met me in the kitchen with her coat and pocketbook and said, "We need to go!" (This is from someone who in over fifty years has never been to an ER and never complains about pain.)

While I was driving at the speed of a NASCAR race to the hospital–somehow avoiding a ticket, she shared between gasps of breath that the pain was worse than giving birth to Jon and Chris. Hours later it was discovered she had a huge kidney stone.

After six days of drinking gallons of water with no relief from the pain the doctors discovered the stone was lodged sideways and would not move. Surgery was scheduled for a week later. Miraculously the stone finally passed–only hours before surgery was scheduled and two weeks following the initial diagnosis.

In addition to physical pain, we have experienced emotional hurt. Disappointments, the loss of someone we love, abuse, or simply hearing unkind words that hurt our feelings can all be a source of emotional pain.

We are familiar with the phrase that someone 'has the patience of Job' so it's important to be reminded what circumstances led to his reputation.

Snapshot Picture of Scripture (Job 1, 42:10, 12)

Job was a very wealthy man and in Old Testament times wealth was often measured in livestock.

He owned seven thousand sheep, three thousand camels, five hundred yoke of oxen, and five hundred donkeys. He also had a large number of household workers, seven sons and three daughters.

One day many of his animals were stolen. Later a fire burned all Job's property, killed all his servants and the other animals. Then a storm knocked down Job's son's house with his children inside and they all died. (And sometimes we think *we* have had a bad day!)

For months he endured intense physical affliction with open sores covering his body. His entire wealth and livelihood were wiped out!

His friends and wife questioned his loyalty to God. Job asked the question many of us ask when tragedy, disappointment or suffering enters our life, "Why me?" Except for Christ, no one in the Bible suffered more than Job.

But through all his pain, suffering and adversity, he remained faithful. After he lost everything Job's positive response is almost unimaginable. Job said, "The LORD gave, and the LORD has taken away; may the name of the LORD be praised" (Job 1:21 NIV).

Pain has a purpose.

When we are experiencing a season of pain it can seem as though nothing positive will possibly come from it. But pain can create a resilience in us that only comes with struggles. The struggle is the proof that there is still hope. And during the struggle is when we really grow. Pain has sort of a sneaky way of pushing us back toward Jesus.

Sometimes God's preparation comes packaged as pain. But don't look at life from the perspective of pain but see your life from the perspective of purpose. Realize that God may be doing something *in you* before He does something *through you.*

The Good News is pain can actually be a gift to us. The great Christian author C.S. Lewis wrote in *The Problem of Pain*, "God whispers to us in our pleasures, speaks to us in our conscience, but shouts in our pain. It is His megaphone to rouse a deaf world."

Pain can be a blessing and a gift.

It may not make sense to us at the time, but pain can also be a blessing. It warns us, corrects us, and guides us. It can bring us back to

Christ when we've taken a detour and lost our way.

God can use what seems like the worst of times in life to bless us the most. He likes to surprise us when we least expect a blessing. Tough times for us is the perfect time for God to do what only He can do.

If we search long enough, we can find a blessing in everything. Behind every experience in your life there is a lesson and a blessing. Pain always leaves a gift.

Pause and ask yourself, "What gift, blessing or lesson did I learn from my last painful experience? What do I do when the pain and suffering won't seem to stop?"

Even though the Apostle Paul prayed several times for God to take his pain away, he learned from the experience and later shared the encouraging words that 'the pain you've been feeling can't compare with the joy that is coming'!

We know better but sometimes we communicate with God only *after* we've talked with everyone else. Or we wait until we experience times of emotional or physical suffering before we turn to Him for help and comfort.

Whatever you have been through or are going through God can use to prepare you for the good that is coming. *There is nothing out of God's redemptive reach. God can make all things new in your life!*

No magic potion for a painful emotion

Many times we discover that emotional pain can seem more difficult to break through than physical pain. In other words 'a broken heart can hurt deeper and longer than a broken bone'.

In times like these when we feel our heart is crushed, we can find comfort and encouragement in the words of David, "The LORD is close to the brokenhearted and saves those who are crushed in spirit" (Psalm 34:18 NIV).

It can also help to share our feelings with family and friends with whom we have confidence. I love the touching story about the little girl who sadly lost her father in a tragic accident. Her mother tried to console her by sharing that their Heavenly Father would take care of them. The little girl responded by saying, "But I need a father with skin on." God loves honesty and desires for us to express our emotions openly with Him.

At my lowest—God is my hope.
At my darkest—God is my light.
At my weakest—God is my strength.
At my saddest—God is my comfort.

Jesus Himself endured the ultimate pain for us so we can be assured God will never leave us. As believers, we have this source of comfort in our pain and the assurance God is always with us.

You've been planted—not buried!

"For I am about to do something new. See, I have already begun!" (Isaiah 43:19 NLT).

The enemy thought Job had lost everything. *But Job's everything* was *God.* When you come up and break through the pain—and you will, you can experience a new season of spring in your life! Get ready because it's coming!

Positive Points to Ponder
- God's purpose for you is greater than your problems or pain.
- God has...
    a reason for your struggles
    a reward for your faithfulness, and
    a purpose for your pain!
    Don't Give Up!

12

Face Your Fears and Defeat Defiant Giants

What's one of my biggest fears? That's an easy question with a simple two-word answer for me—roller coasters. They absolutely scare me into a total state of fright.

I still break into a cold sweat recalling my surrender to peer pressure from a group of students on a school trip to Kings Dominion. The name should have told me not to even consider riding it. With a three-hundred-foot drop at an eighty-five degree angle, it was known as *The Extreme Intimidator*.

Squeezing the safety bar in front of me so tightly that my knuckles turned white from the lack of blood flow. And the only time I slightly opened my eyes, I thought we were literally going to leave the track and shoot into outer space with no parachute.

During the ride I caught up with all the prayer times I had skipped during my life. And I made many promises to God including that if He would bring me safely to the ground, I would willingly leave immediately to be a missionary anywhere in the world.

Last year our family visited Dollywood. Having learned a lesson from my past experience, while the adults and older grandkids, Sienna and Carson, rode the 20 stories high *Lightning Rod*, I rode the Kiddie Coaster with our then three and four-year-old grandsons, Anderson and Malachi. At only three months old, if Sam had been with us, I feel certain he would have joined me in the back car.

How about you? What is one of your biggest fears? Looking under the bed in the dark when you were a kid? Flying? Speaking in public?

One of the challenges of familiarity with scripture is sometimes we tend to close our hearts and minds to new insights we can learn. The story of David and Goliath contains several life-lessons about overcoming fear and demonstrating courage during challenging times.

Snapshot Picture of Scripture (1 Samuel 17)

As outlined in the traditional Hebrew text, the Philistines and the Israelites each occupied a hill on opposite sides of a valley ready for battle. Goliath, a giant representing the Philistines, would threaten the Israelites every day, but they were afraid, and no one would fight him.

But David, a shepherd boy, was filled with faith and a passion for God's name which was being blasphemed. As a shepherd he was a skilled slinger and protected his sheep daily from wild animals.

Visualize the nine-foot tall giant Goliath standing in full armor as young five-foot tall David comes toward him with a slingshot and five stones he picked up from the creek.

David knew God was with him and confidently ran to the laughing and intimidating Goliath who mistakenly underestimated the little shepherd boy. With both armies watching, David calmly put a stone in his sling and hit Goliath in the forehead right between his eyes and killed him.

And what did the Philistines do after they watched their defiant giant be destroyed? Like most bullies when someone courageously stands up to them—they turned and ran.

Face Your Fears

Everyone fears something. It is interesting that the fear of public speaking is not included on the latest list of top phobias compiled by leading psychologists:
- Social Phobias—excessive self-consciousness (number one fear)
- Acrophobia—fear of heights
- Claustrophobia—fear of enclosed places
- Ophidiophobia—fear of snakes
- Atychiphobia—fear of failure
- Coasterphobia—fear of roller coasters (It's good to know there is a name for at least one of my problems.)

The word *fear* itself can create fear for some people. Our perspective can influence the extent to which we are afraid. For instance, we can view it as; **F**ear **E**verything **A**nd **R**un. Or **F**ace **E**verything **A**nd **R**ise. The latter describes David's perspective.

I don't believe it's a coincidence that there is an instruction in scripture appearing in some form 365 times: ***Do not be afraid.*** In other words, we could read a different verse every day for a year telling us not to fear.

David later wrote, "I prayed to the Lord, and he answered me. He freed me from all my fears" (Psalm 34:4 NLT).

God wired our brains to experience fear. It is a primary emotion. There is a reason and purpose for our fear as we respond to triggering stimuli. When God tells us not to fear, He isn't commanding us to shut off part of our brain.

The real issue in dealing with fear is where do we go when we fear. God invites us to come to Him. He can help us take the next step of faith even in the middle of our fear.

When we become followers of Christ, He never promises us life will be a cake walk. Actually, He told us to take up our cross—which is sometimes heavy and scary—and follow Him.

Our Christian journey may seem like signing up for a trip with a travel agency. But we can't just register for the Fun and Fellowship Package. We also have to include the Trials and Tribulations Travel Special.

We tend to allow our circumstances to come between God and us instead of putting God between us and our circumstances. We know in our hearts that He is bigger than any problem but still find ourselves in situations that lead to fearing the outcome. We must constantly trust Him to help keep our faith bigger than our fear.

David had no military experience, no armor and no sword—just a slingshot and some rocks from the creek. But he knew God was with him. Instead of focusing on *how*, he focused on *who* and Goliath came tumbling down.

God chose David and He chose *you*!

We know David became a great leader but sometimes need to be reminded how he was chosen. Jesse was David's father and Samuel came to his house to anoint and choose the next king. One by one David's brothers were all brought before Samuel. Each was very impressive but after seeing them Samuel turned to Jesse and asked if there were any others.

Jesse shared that his youngest son was just a teen and outside—probably watching the sheep or playing music on his harp. Samuel requested they go get him.

When David walked in the room with his seven older brothers staring, Samuel took one look and immediately exclaimed, "This is him! This is him! This is the one I will anoint!"

Don't miss this important part of the story. Jesse left the kid outside and Samuel had to send for him to come into the house. I sometimes wonder what David's story would be if Samuel hadn't asked for the little teenage shepherd boy to come inside.

You may not look like something special. You may have messed up big-time. You may not think you were chosen by God to do anything extraordinary. But I will assure you that He chose you to do something for Him—possibly right where you are!

How to Defeat Your Defiant Giants

Whatever *giants* you may be dealing with, you can learn how to defeat them through lessons from David.

He remembered past victories. Since God had helped him be victorious in the past with lions and bears, he knew God would help him in the present. Focus on challenges in which God helped you through.

He realized personal assets. Goliath was huge compared to David. But David knew that God had the power to defeat the giant, so he used the asset God provided—a sling and five stones. You have assets like determination and persistence, so don't give up.

He relied on a powerful God. Goliath had size, strength, and a sword but David came in the name of the Lord. Always remember how big your God is.

Fear can be the greatest barrier to us fulfilling God's plan for our lives. God hasn't given us a spirit of fear but a spirit of love. "There is no fear in love, but perfect love casts out fear" (1 John 4:13a NRSV).

When you love God and know you belong to Him, you can defeat any giant. No giant you are facing, or will face, is too big for Him—no sickness too painful, no addiction too powerful, no relationship too heart-breaking, no obstacle too big or strong! With Him anything is possible!

Positive Points to Ponder
- If God puts a Goliath in front of you, He must believe you have a David inside of you. Make a decision today to choose faith over fear!
- Don't be afraid of tomorrow because God is already there waiting on you!

13

Strong and Courageous Can Be Contagious

If you were asked to reflect about someone you personally know who experienced major challenges in life and showed amazing strength and courage, who comes to mind?

I can think of several, including my mother who battled cancer for many years. And my sister Ronda who also courageously lived a life of physical and emotional challenges.

She was a senior in high school when my mom called and shared that Ronda was having severe pains throughout her body the doctors couldn't explain. She spent time at several medical facilities and their specialists couldn't agree on a diagnosis. After several frustrating months she was accepted to NIH (National Institutes of Health).

The phenomenal staff at NIH diagnosed her with the life-challenging disease Systemic Lupus Erythematosus. Lupus is now more common, but in the early 1970's it was extremely rare. In addition to the excruciating pain, it dramatically weakened her immune system and bones.

Through the following years she endured multiple operations resulting in replacing both knees and both hips and she spent much of her time either in a wheelchair or on crutches.

In spite of all her continuous setbacks, she physically attended college—no online classes—earned a four-year college degree and was appropriately employed at a hospital helping others through tough times.

The last several years of her life were spent in a nursing home where she continued to demonstrate her contagious strength and faith in God. After a 28-year courageous battle, Ronda passed at the early age of 46.

There is a leader in the Old Testament who encountered a different kind of challenge in his life but also demonstrated how to *be strong and courageous.*

Snapshot Picture of Scripture (Joshua 1:7-9; 6:12-20)

Joshua lived under slavery in Egypt for 40 years, then wandered through the wilderness another 40 years as Moses' assistant. After Moses died, Joshua was appointed by God at the prime age of 80 to lead the people across the Jordan River to Cana and eventually capture the city of Jericho.

The Hebrew name Joshua–Yeshua, is the same Greek name for Jesus, meaning 'salvation has come'. The command to 'Be strong and courageous' is mentioned 25 times in scripture and four times in these first nine verses of Joshua.

Can you imagine following in the footsteps of the great leader Moses? It's difficult to comprehend the high level of pressure the new leader Joshua experienced.

If visualized in the perspective of today's sports leadership, that would be more stressful than getting hired as a head coach after the previous coach had won forty consecutive national championships. That would be some serious tennis shoes to fill.

Before God is finished, He gives Joshua a couple of additional bonus commands and the reason for believing and obeying. "Be strong and courageous. Do not be afraid; Do not be discouraged, for the LORD your God will be with you wherever you go" (Joshua 1:9 NIV).

As many times as God reminds us He will be with us, it must be a little perplexing to Him when we seem to constantly forget and need to be reminded. *Not only is He with us wherever we go but He's already there!*

"Keep on keeping on."

Dr. Helen Roseveare became a Christian while a medical student at Cambridge. After graduation she followed her calling to be a medical missionary in the Congo. While living in an old leprosy camp, she built hospitals and training centers.

In 1964 she was taken prisoner by rebel forces enduring beatings and multiple rapes. She was finally released and headed back home for a brief time before returning to the Congo to rebuild hospitals that had been destroyed.

In a video titled *Mama Luka Comes Home,* Dr. Roseveare shares a moving story about the prayer of a 10-year-old African girl and her experience to save a premature newborn baby.

As people gathered around Dr. Roseveare's bed during her last days, she was asked what message she would like to share. She replied, "Keep on keeping on." What a simple and profound way to remind us to 'be strong and courageous'!

And now the rest of the story...
Recognize that God brought you to where you are for a reason.

God prepared Joshua for the biggest mission of his life by doing the little things first. Whatever you're doing now may seem insignificant, but you may be in training so you will be prepared when a new or different opportunity arises.

We may not express it verbally, but we have a tendency to question why things happen as they do. This can be dangerous as it may result in holding back and not taking action on what needs to be done.

Similar to jumping in a pool. There are times we need to check the temperature of the water by reaching down and touching it. Then there are times we just need to take a big breath, jump off the board and do a cannonball!

Step out in faith and get your feet wet.

The Jordan River usually flows slowly and is calm. But scripture tells us it was harvest time and it was at flood stage. Scholars believe it could have been 100 feet wide and 10 feet deep when over 2 million people crossed through it on dry land!

We aren't sure why this happened while the Jordan River was at its most dangerous stage. Any other time they could have just walked across. I believe it was because *they would have missed the miracle*! God leads us with cords of kindness to overwhelming circumstances precisely to show us His power and glory.

Many times we want to wait until the situation is perfect. But the people stepped in the water *before* it stopped flowing. Be strong and courageous and prayerfully take a step before you know the outcome, before all the details have been worked out. We should plan and seek God's guidance when making decisions, but at some point, stop standing on the bank. Take a step and get your feet wet!

Believe your wall will fall!

After everyone crossed the Jordan, another step of courage was to believe if they followed God's promise, they could take the city of Jericho. But the plan God gave Joshua seemed ridiculous.

The city was surrounded by huge walls 25 feet high and 20 feet thick. But instead of the Israelite army attacking the city and taking it by force, God had another plan. The army was to walk around the city one time each day for six days with the priests blowing their trumpets. Say what? That's right–just march around the city and play their horns.

On the seventh day they were to walk around the city seven times and then when Joshua gave the command everyone was to shout. Can you picture the men standing on top of the city walls with their weapons drawn ready for combat as they watched this strange procession?

The result of Joshua following God's command is found in Joshua 6:20. "...when the men gave a loud shout, the wall collapsed, so everyone charged straight in, and they took the city."

Key Question: What wall in your life have you been hoping and praying will fall? *Trust God*, even when it doesn't make sense and you look foolish to others–like priests playing trumpets as they march around a city wall. *Have courage and be strong and you can't go wrong!*

Positive Points to Ponder
- With God you are braver than you believe, stronger than you seem, and smarter than you think.
- Courage doesn't always roar. Sometimes courage is God's quiet voice at the end of the day that simply says 'I'm still here. Try again tomorrow'.

14

Dealing With Difficult, Disagreeable People

Be honest. When you read the chapter title you almost instantaneously thought of someone you've encountered who fits the categories of *difficult and/or disagreeable*.

Let's be honest. Not everyone is easy to like. When we only have one nerve left, they seem to find a way to get on it. Or as someone has shared, some people brighten the room when they walk in. Others when they walk out.

The person who appears on my memory radar was one of my former supervisors. Apparently, her mission in life was to make everyone she came in contact with as miserable as possible. It was on my daily to-do list to shine some light in her darkness by saying or doing something that resulted in seeing at least a partial smile on her face. An actual laugh was rare and an extra blessing.

On one occasion I wished her Happy Birthday, and she responded by sharing that birthdays mean we are getting older. "So why should I be happy about getting older?"

Many believe it's good that we can always look at followers of Christ in the Bible as positive examples of people who didn't argue or disagree, right? Not so fast my friend.

Actually, we don't need to look further than the apostles. They spent the most time with Jesus during His ministry and personally heard His teachings about loving each other on a daily basis.

But on at least one occasion, the reason for their arguing and disagreeing has a very similar sound. Read closely and see if you know anyone, kids or adults, who may use different words but ask the same questions about their importance.

Snapshot Picture of Scripture (Luke 22:23-27)

After serving the disciples bread and wine at the Last Supper, Jesus shared that one of them would betray Him. They were shocked and asked each other who would do such a terrible thing?

The discussion turned into an argument about who would be the greatest among them in the kingdom of God. Jesus shared that usually the people sitting at the table are considered more important than the servers. Then He explained that the one who serves is actually the greatest.

Let's look at a few observations about the disciples before focusing on some valuable life lessons.

Firstly, the simple fact the disciples argued. Can you imagine being in Jesus' sandals? He shared that He would be crucified the next day, and His closest followers got into an argument.

I would be thinking something like, "Heavenly Father, You've got to be kidding me. After teaching these guys every day for three years about humility and love, *this* is how my time on earth will end?"

Secondly, they were arguing about who would be the most important in the kingdom. I can only imagine them sharing their personal reasons why they deserve to be considered the greatest, the most important, who gets to sit the closest to Christ.

Lastly, the true colors of their heart and different personalities came to the surface. I imagine some of them remained relatively quiet, and some were more vocal in expressing themselves. It became obvious they were different in how they behaved and communicated.

Different is not bad—different is just…different.

There is nothing more important than our relationship with God and others. And how we communicate demonstrates our different behavior tendencies with which we are born. To establish positive relationships with and understand others, we must first understand ourselves.

Why do I tend to speak a certain way, argue, or disagree? Why do we have a tendency to react in a specific way most of the time? Why do some people seem to remain calm and listen while others are bolder and sometimes disagreeable?

Paul tells us in Colossians to 'get along with each other, forgive each other, and love each other'. And in his letter to the folk in Ephesus 'don't say anything corrupt or negative but build each other up with positive words'.

Ever been driving in the right lane and decided to pass the vehicle in front of you? After checking both the side and rearview mirrors and it seems clear, you turn on your signal light and start to pass. But seemingly out of nowhere there is a vehicle beside you and immediately you return to the right lane. They were in your *blind spot.*

Since we all have personal blind spots and can't see 'the real me', it's helpful to look at the *Biblical DISC Personal Profile.* It is an instrument used by thousands world-wide. As a certified DISC trainer, I have found it enhances communication skills and relationships by understanding ourselves. And it has the added bonus of studying different kinds of behavior tendencies in a Christian Biblical context.

Each of us is made up of some of all four categories. Enjoy looking at the descriptions below and *honestly* see if one or two describe your behavior tendencies a little more than the others.

Flashback to an instant replay of the disagreeable conversation of the disciples. Find any personality similarities of the disciples to anyone you know?

D–Determined, **D**emanding, **D**oer (*The Apostle Paul*): high amount of self-confidence and enjoys being in charge, highly energetic. If you want something done, give the job to a 'high D' person. (Before he became a follower of Christ, Paul was a terrorist to Christians. After his conversion he served God with everything in his being.)

I–Influential, **I**nspirational, **I**nteractive (*The Apostle Peter*): considered a people person, outspoken, loves to talk and socialize, sometimes speaks before thinking. If you want someone to encourage others or speak in front of the group, call on a 'high I' person. (When the disciples saw Jesus walking on water, who was the first to blurt out and ask if he could walk on the water, too?)

S–Steadfast, **S**upportive, **S**ervant (*The Apostle John*): loves to listen and help people, loyal, doesn't like conflict or attention, and humbly puts others before themselves. If you want a loving, caring person who will listen to problems, go to a 'high S' person. (Even though he wrote the Gospel of John, you won't find one place in the entire book where he mentions his own name.)

C–Calculating, **C**ompetent, **C**orrect (*The Apostle Matthew*): takes pride in making sure the task is done right. If you want someone to keep accurate records, submit a report before the deadline, or check for errors, ask the 'high C' person. (When Jesus called him to be a follower, Matthew was a tax collector and kept detailed financial records for the Roman government.)

The starting point of handling disagreeable people is understanding yourself. Knowing and being aware of how people communicate, using the DISC descriptions, can help your relationship with them. When the disciples argued, Jesus knew their hearts and reacted according to each follower's behavior tendencies.

A little DISC humor helps humanize our hindrances.

When we don't understand why people act the way they do, in essence we are asking, 'Why can't everyone act like me'? Let's exaggerate DISC a little to make a point that it is good we are different.

4 People Go Grocery Shopping:

The 'high D' likes to be in charge and might approach someone they don't know and tell them where a certain item is without being asked. The 'high I' likes to talk and might leave the store with no groceries but made 3 new friends.

The 'high S' likes to help others and might offer to take two or three customers' groceries to their car. The 'high C' keeps accurate records and not only uses coupons but has the total amount calculated with the discounts before the cashier finishes.

Use Jesus' example to handle arguments and disagreements.
1. ***Know yourself.*** Jesus understood who He was and His purpose on earth. Know who you are, what you believe, and why you're here. Basic life questions to which everyone needs to pursue the answers.
2. ***Communicate and establish relationships.*** Jesus created relationships by spending time with His followers, fans, and fanatical nonbelievers—who loved to argue. When people know you respect them even though you may not agree with their beliefs, they are more likely to listen when attempting to share.
3. ***Demonstrate agape love.*** Literally love others unconditionally. That is easier to say or write than to do. It is a tough task but that's the example Jesus gave us. When the disciples started arguing, He kept His cool and didn't tell them they were wrong or to stop.

Understanding and practicing that we don't have to prove we are right in every situation and truly love others is a huge hurdle when handling difficult, disagreeable people. How do we do that? By following Christ's example of love–which binds our community with a double-dose of unity!

Positive Points to Ponder
- Arguments usually last too long because one person is too stubborn to forgive and the other too proud to apologize. Be the person who breaks the code and demonstrates love.
- Obviously, both parties believe they are right or there wouldn't be an argument at all. Our situation or experiences in life may cause us to see things differently from another who has had different experiences. If two people are looking at a 6, but one of them is standing on the opposite side of the paper, it may appear to be a 9 to them. Same paper, same printed number, but two perspectives. Be the one to accept the other person's perspective even if you see it differently.

15

It's Hard to Be Humble When You're Perfect

Researching opposites for the word *humble* and found: arrogant, egotistical, superior, and conceited. Just the kind of person we enjoy spending time with, right?

If no one who fits that description comes to mind perhaps the lyrics to the song written and recorded by Mac Davis, *Oh Lord It's Hard to Be Humble When You're Perfect In Every Way*, might help clarify:

> Oh Lord, it's hard to be humble,
> when you're perfect in every way,
> I can't wait to look in the mirror,
> 'cause I get better looking each day;
> To know me is to love me,
> I must be a heck of a man,
> Oh Lord, it's hard to be humble,
> but I'm doing the best that I can.

In the previous chapter we discovered the disciples started arguing about who among them would be the greatest in the Kingdom of God. What Jesus did next to teach them the real meaning of humility was almost unprecedented for anyone—especially a rabbi.

Snapshot Picture of Scripture (John 13:1-5)
Jesus and His disciples were eating the Passover meal, and He surprised them when He got up and wrapped a towel around His waist. He then poured water into a basin, and much to the amazement of the disciples, one-by-one He knelt in front of each and washed and dried their feet.

Why washing the disciples' feet was (and is) a big deal.

People wore sandals or walked barefooted on the roads in Palestine during the first century, making it imperative that feet be washed before a meal. It was customary in most homes to provide a water basin at the door. When visitors entered, they either washed their own feet or a servant would be assigned the task. People reclined at a low table while eating and their feet were clearly visible.

When Jesus rose from the table and began to wash the feet of the disciples, He was taking on the role of the lowliest of servants. They must have been shocked into silence at this unheard-of demonstration of humility and love. Jesus, their Lord, Master, and Rabbi did what *they* should have done.

Pause and allow that thought to soak in. Jesus washed Simon Peter's feet, who would publicly deny he knew Him in the next 24 hours. More shocking, He washed the feet of Judas Iscariot, the one who would betray Him. Visualize when Jesus humbly knelt at his feet and looked up as their eyes met—both knowing what would happen.

What would you do if you knew tomorrow would be your last day on earth? I would communicate and spend as much time as possible with people I love. Jesus knew and what did He do? He washed His friends' feet!

The paradox of greatness: They had been arguing about who would be the greatest. *The formula for greatness is service.* Jesus shared that when we can serve at the highest level those who are perceived to be at the lowest level, that is the sign of greatness. Not congratulations, recognition, applause, being put in the spotlight or given an impressive title.

Those are the things some of his followers, then and now, believe demonstrate greatness. But His simple, humble action of washing feet was saying, **"Give up the title and grab a towel."** We may not look cool or be popular serving with a towel, but it is literally what Jesus did.

Jesus came to the earth, not as a king and conqueror, but as a suffering servant. "Even as the Son of Man came not to be served but to serve" (Matthew 20:28a ESV).

Let's look at the elephant (or feet) in the room. Feet are not pretty. They have toenails, calluses, and hard heels. I don't know about you, but I don't even want to look at someone's feet—much less touch them. Have you ever seen proud parents showing pictures of their baby's feet? Or when describing a new relationship, ever heard the person say,

"And you should see her feet. They are gorgeous."

In all sincerity, what really moves me emotionally is the thought that in less than 24 hours after this event, the same two hands that washed and dried the disciples' stinking, dirty feet would have nails driven in them–*for you and me*. Pause and reflect on that thought.

It All Depends On Whose Hands It's In

If I hold a basketball in my hands, it's worth about $15.00. When Michael Jordan held a basketball, it was worth millions. If I hold a slingshot in my hands, it's worth about $10.00. When David held a slingshot, he defeated a nine-foot giant. If I hold a few slices of bread in my hands, I can make a couple of PB&J sandwiches and feed two or three people. When Jesus broke bread, He fed over 5,000. It all depends on whose hands it's in.

Most importantly, if I hold a couple of nails and some wood in my hands, I could possibly make a really bad bird house. *But put two nails and some wood in Jesus' hands and the cross leads to His physical death so we could live with Him forever. You see,* **it all depends on whose hands it's in!**

Lessons to learn from washing and drying filthy feet.

Ignore pride, position, and power and do whatever needs to be done to serve others. Don't let pride make you hide. It can prohibit us from stepping up and out to serve with humility of heart. Follow the example of Christ and be willing to get your hands dirty. James tells us that God will resist the proud but give grace to the humble.

Be grateful for the opportunity to serve. Look at serving with a mindset of thankfulness instead of as a responsibility. Think of all the humble deeds people have done for you.

Put humility and servanthood into action. Don't just pray for opportunities–actively look for them and you'll find plenty. Write or text an encouraging note, call someone, deliver a meal, visit someone, hold the door for someone, pay for the person's order in line behind you…*just develop a mindset to daily do something to humbly serve others.*

Positive Points to Ponder
- Pride builds walls between people. Humility builds bridges.
- Humility is not thinking less of yourself. It is thinking of yourself less.

16

Life's Toughest Tests Can Bring Out Your Best

One of the most dreaded things a teacher could say to me was, "I have your parents' phone number and will be calling them tonight." And number two on the list went something like, "Everyone please put your books under your desk, get out a sheet of paper and number from one to ten. This pop quiz will count as a test grade." (It suddenly occurred to me that maybe I should have completed the homework assignment last night instead of watching a ball game.)

Perhaps you remember hearing the following words years ago on television or radio: "This is a test of the Emergency Broadcasting System. We repeat, this is only a test. If this were an actual emergency, you would be given further instructions." This notice of a test was followed by an ear-piercing tone that truly tested my level of tolerance for headaches.

Life is full of tests that are more serious than a pop quiz in class or on the airwaves. In fact, life itself is a test. The Bible contains many events that occur 40 times and usually it represents a time of testing and growing.

In the Old Testament we find the amazing story of a father being given the ultimate test—to sacrifice his son.

Snapshot Picture of Scripture (Genesis 22:1-19)
Abraham and Isaac made the three-day trip to the designated place on the mountain and started carrying the wood for the sacrificial offering. During their walk together Isaac asked his father where the lamb was for the burnt offering. Abraham shared that God would supply the sacrifice.

Isaac was unaware that God had asked Abraham to sacrifice *him* to be the sacrifice. When they reached their destination Abraham made an altar and arranged the wood on it. Then he bound Isaac, laid him on the altar, and raised his knife to slay him.

But as soon as he raised his hand to do the unthinkable, an angel interrupted and told him not to lay a hand on his son. Abraham saw a ram caught in the bushes, so he took the ram and sacrificed it instead of his son.

Look at the story with different eyes.

Walk a mile in Isaac's shoes. Actually, scholars estimate it was a challenging hike of about 50 miles. So, he's walking with his dad for about three days without having a clue what Abraham intends to do. Isaac is over twenty years old, so when the time came there is a good possibility he willingly allowed Abraham to bind him on the altar.

Can you imagine Isaac's huge sigh of relief when his dad took him off the altar and replaced him with the ram for the burnt offering? I would have enjoyed being a bird in the bushes listening to their conversation during the return walk down the mountain as Isaac possibly told Abraham he had some explaining to do.

And how about Sarah? This passage doesn't tell us that Abraham shared his plans with her. But if he did, I would guess that conversation would have lasted a while. "When you get to the top of the mountain, you're going to do *what*?" They had waited twenty-five years for Sarah to become pregnant and both were now over a hundred years old. Isaac was definitely a miracle baby and a very special son.

The difference between tests and temptations.

Temptations. The purpose of temptation is to bring out the worst in us and for us to learn to overcome. Fortunately God is our partner, and if we choose, He promises to bring us victory in the middle of our temptation.

"No temptation has overtaken you except what is common to man. And God is faithful; He will not let you be tempted beyond what you can bear" (1 Corinthians 10:13a ESV).

Author and theologian C. S. Lewis shares, "A silly idea is current that good people do not know what temptation means. This is an obvious lie. Only those who try to resist temptation know how strong it is. A person who gives in to temptation after five minutes simply does not know what it would have been like an hour later."

Tests. God is the source of all tests. One of the purposes of tests in life is so we can learn whether or not we can apply the lessons of living a Godly life. We all experience different kinds of tests; emotional, physical, financial, mental, relational, and spiritual. Tests also help reveal our character.

James says it like this, "When troubles of any kind come your way, consider it an opportunity for great joy. For you know that when your faith is tested, your endurance has a chance to grow" (James 1:2-3 NLT).

Dr. Roger Barrier makes these observations and points out that when God told Abraham to sacrifice his son, it wasn't the first time his faith was tested. His life was filled with multiple tests: the famine test, the flock test, the fortune test, and the family test.

And author Rick Warren shares, "When you understand that life is a test, you realize that nothing is insignificant in your life. Even the smallest incident has significance for you. The ultimate test of faith is not how loudly you praise God in happy times, but how deeply you trust Him in dark times."

How to make the honor roll and pass life's tests.

What is the most challenging academic test you've taken? Standardized test in school, ACT or SAT for college acceptance, ASVAB for placement in the armed forces, or graduate school acceptance or completion exam?

Abraham took and passed the ultimate final exam. His test was to show his Heavenly Father the strength of his faith and he demonstrated trust by his willingness to sacrifice his one and only son. Sounds familiar to the Easter story, doesn't it?

In order to receive all that God has, we must be willing to give all that we have. Abraham was willing to give up his son to follow God and receive His blessings. As the story ends, we see that God's plan wasn't for the sacrifice but to see if Abraham's heart was willing to do so.

Stay strong and courageous. The Good News—there will be situations and people that will test your faith. But if you stay strong and trust in God you will be rewarded.

"Blessed is the man who remains steadfast under trial, for when he has stood the test he will receive the crown of life" (James 1:12 ESV).

Scholars have drawn several striking parallels between the story of Isaac and his earthly father with Jesus and his Heavenly Father:

- Isaac, like Jesus, was miraculously conceived. (Sarah was ninety years old and had been barren her entire life.)

- Isaac was his father's beloved son. Jesus was His Heavenly Father's beloved Son.
- Isaac carried the wood for his own sacrifice. Jesus carried His own wooden cross to be sacrificed.
- The journey to Mount Moriah took three days—the same amount of time Jesus was in the tomb before His resurrection.
- The most intriguing comparison—Mount Moriah, the place where Abraham was prepared to sacrifice his son, is the exact same place, (Golgotha), where two thousand years later God sacrificed His Son, Jesus!

Understand that your faith will not instantly deliver you *from* every test in life. But your faith will carry you *through* every test. And He is using what you have experienced and are going through right now to prepare you for the blessings to come!

Positive Points to Ponder
- Opportunity knocks only once, but tests and temptations lean on the doorbell.
- You can't have a *message* without going through a *mess* and you can't have a *testimony* without a *test*!

17

Real Living Begins with Forgiving

One of the most widely recognizable names in recent history synonymous with forgiveness is Nelson Mandela. His Christian lifestyle of love, reconciliation and forgiveness is rare.

He boldly took a public stand against Apartheid—a policy and practice of segregation and discrimination against the non-white majority in the republic of South Africa.

He was incarcerated in a maximum-security prison for twenty-eight years, much of the time enduring horrific living conditions in a seven foot cell with a slop bucket. He was treated harshly by the prison personnel, was allowed no reading material, and crushed stone all day to make gravel.

But instead of revenge and retribution he chose to forgive and made peace with his captors and jailors. Mandela shared, "Forgiveness liberates the soul and removes fear. That's why it's such a powerful weapon."

One of the most powerful stories Jesus shared about forgiveness is the parable of the Prodigal Son.

Snapshot Picture of Scripture. (Luke 15:11-32)

A man had two sons and the youngest asked his father to give him his share of the estate. To everyone's surprise his father agreed. The son soon packed his bags, took his inheritance, and left home.

He enjoyed a lifestyle of party-hardy and eventually blew all his money on wild living. A famine came, and since he had lost everything, the only job he could find was feeding pigs.

He had nothing to eat, no money, no friends, and no mercy from anyone. He finally decided to face up to his mistakes, return home, humbly ask his father to forgive him and offer to be one of his servants.

His father had been patiently waiting for his return. When he saw his son from a distance, he ran to him, interrupting the forgiveness speech his son had prepared. He hugged him and began instructing the servants to give him the best sandals, the best robe, the best ring and the best meal!

Feeding filthy pigs is far from fun.
The youngest son received one third of the estate. To ask for his share before his father died was insulting and disrespectful. It implied he wished his father was dead. But as surprising as the son's request for the estate is the fact that his father agreed to give it to him.

According to the book of Leviticus, pigs were considered an unclean animal, and Jews were not allowed to eat or touch them. So, feeding pigs was the most detestable, disgraceful job a Jew could possibly have. He must have been desperately at the end of his rope with no other options available to take a job feeding them.

When he realized what a monumental mistake he made and without knowing if his father would accept him, he started practicing his apology speech. He was in for a super surprise for his welcome home!

"We'll leave the light on."
Jon, Chris, and their families both live out of town, and sometimes before a visit they will share that they will be arriving late. To which we always respond, 'we'll leave the light on'.

In this parable I can visualize the father sitting on his front porch day after day, anxiously waiting and anticipating his son's return home. And when it's time to retire each evening, he reluctantly looks down the road one last time before going to bed.

He then lights a lamp just in case his son shows up during the night. This ritual continues for a long time, but his father never gives up hope. One evening he sees someone at a distance, and jumping from his chair he squints until he finally recognizes his son. It's him! His son who was lost is now found!

In an amazing demonstration of love his father doesn't wait for him on the porch. Scripture says he *ran* to greet him. I love the visual of the father jumping off the porch, pulling up his robe, (which was completely unacceptable in Jewish culture), and sprinting toward his son as fast as he could run.

He proudly tells everyone it's time to celebrate. Why? Because his son that was considered dead is now alive again—was lost and is now found!

If you've waited for someone to return after an extended time, how did you respond when they returned? Many would respond as this father by preparing their favorite meal, talking, and laughing about old times deep into the night.

Lessons Learned from A Forgiving, Faithful Father:

We sometimes focus so much on the prodigal son's actions, we miss the amazing grace, mercy, and forgiveness of his loving father. Actually, the word *prodigal*, meaning wasteful or reckless, doesn't appear in the original text of the Bible.

There was also an older son who decided to be loyal, stay on the farm, and continue working for his father. He became jealous when everyone celebrated the return of his younger brother. Do you know anyone who may have responded in a similar manner?

Let's clarify the difference between some of the Christian traits his father lovingly demonstrated:

- *Grace* - undeserved favor; the aspect of God's love that gives us what we do *not* deserve. After his actions, the son did not deserve the welcome he received.
- *Mercy* - compassion; the aspect of God's love that withholds punishment that we *do* deserve. Grace and mercy are two sides of the coin of God's love. His father could have disowned him, demanding repayment of his inheritance.
- *Forgiveness* - an intentional decision to let go of resentment or anger. Mercy takes us to the path of forgiveness while grace leads to reconciliation.

"For by grace you have been saved through faith" (Ephesians 2:8a NKJV).

Name That Tune: In 1748 John Newton, a slave trader, was steering his ship filled with slaves through a fierce thunderstorm when he prayed to God for help. After he made it through the storm he attributed his safety to the *grace* of God.

Realizing he was living a life in darkness and was spiritually blind, he asked for *forgiveness*, became a believer, and later a minister and songwriter.

He wrote several hymns including one of the classics–*Amazing Grace*. Reflect on his story of forgiveness, grace and returning home as you read these familiar words:

Amazing Grace, how sweet the sound,
That saved a wretch like me.
I once was lost, but now I'm found,
Was blind, but now I see.

The father of the prodigal son demonstrated grace, mercy, and forgiveness for us.

For Jesus to forgive us, we must forgive others.
That's a strong statement but is specifically stated in scripture. Matthew shares in chapter six that our relationship with God will be damaged if we refuse to forgive those who have offended us.

Peter asked Jesus if we should forgive others up to seven times. Jesus answered, "Not seven, but seventy times seven."

Author and Rabbi Jason Sobel, who is a believer and follower of the Messiah (Yeshua), shares some intriguing insights about these numbers.

Hebrew is an alphanumeric language, meaning each letter has a numeric value. Not only does the number seven mean complete or perfect, but the Hebrew word for 490 also means complete and perfect. We cannot be complete in our faith unless we learn to forgive.

The Hebrew word for Bethlehem, where the Messiah was born, equals 490. He came to bring forgiveness, and the Passover Lamb sacrificed in the temple had to be perfect and complete. In Hebrew, the perfect Passover Lamb equals 490, the word Nativity equals 490, and Bethlehem, which means 'House of Bread', equals 490. Physically and spiritually, we cannot live without the Bread of Forgiveness. Christ extends to us forgiveness so we can be set free to forgive others!

Our Heavenly Father not only waits for us but pursues us until we return. Everything the father commanded his servants to provide for the celebration meant true forgiveness and restoration to the family.

The best robe was a sign of dignity, the ring was a sign of sonship, the sandals a sign of not being a servant, and fatted calves were saved for special feasts. This wasn't just *any* party but a once-in-a-lifetime, dance-the-night-away special celebration.

Forgiving is hard–*really* hard. But I encourage you to join me in acknowledging and praying for anyone who needs to be forgiven—whether they ask or not. Then celebrate your freedom. Most of us don't celebrate spiritual attributes enough. Don't miss the opportunity to follow forgiveness with a personal celebration!

Positive Points to Ponder
- We have to forgive people. We don't have to like them or send them a text message with cute little hearts. But we have to forgive them. If we don't, the rocks of unforgiveness tied around our heart will become so heavy we will never truly live. *Real living begins with forgiving.*
- Before Nelson Mandela left prison he said:
"As I stand before the door to my freedom, I realize that if I do not leave my pain, anger and bitterness behind me, I will still be in prison." *To forgive is to set a prisoner free and then discover that the prisoner was you!*

18

Bloom Where You Are Planted

Recent research states the average American will change careers five to seven times and 30% of the workforce will change jobs every 12 months. *(U.S. Department of Labor)* I decided to jot down my personal list and was surprised at the number—including full and part-time employment:

Dishwasher	Custodian
Furniture Salesman	Fast Food Cook
Karate Instructor	Rock Band Musician
Gas Station Attendant	Clothing Salesman
Grounds Maintenance	Construction Laborer
Finance Co. Collections Mgr.	Training/Speaking Co. (Owner)
Fitness Center (Owner)	Ice Cream Franchise (Owner)
Church Youth Director	Pastor
Public School Educator (Teacher, Counselor, Adm.)	

Stated positively, I have a very *diverse* employment background. One personal observation is that about 70% of my 50+ years of employment was spent in some capacity in the fields of teaching, speaking, pastoring, training, or leading.

People tend to unconsciously judge others based on job titles, education, socio-economic status, age, and many other labels.

We are reminded in a familiar story in Scripture when Jesus fed more than five thousand people with a little boy's lunch that the most ordinary person can be used by Him to accomplish extraordinary things.

Except for the resurrection this is the only miracle recorded in all four gospels. And John is the only writer who includes the important detail of who provided the necessary meal for this miraculous event with the multitudes.

Snapshot Picture of Scripture. (John 6:1-13)

`Jesus had been teaching and healing and a huge crowd followed Him. He asked Phillip, one of His disciples, where the people could buy some food. Philip replied that it would cost more than they could afford.

Then Andrew spoke up and shared that a boy had five barley loaves and two small fish, but it wouldn't be nearly enough to feed this huge crowd.

Jesus asked the disciples to tell everyone to sit down—about 5,000. He took the loaves and the fish, gave thanks, and then miraculously distributed them to the people. They ate as much as they wanted until they were completely full.

Then Jesus told them to take up any leftovers and when they finished the scraps filled 12 baskets!

A little lunch and a lot of faith.

The lunch: The crowd of thousands was hungry. Five small barley loaves and two small fish didn't seem like much. This wasn't exactly a seafood platter special with hushpuppies and slaw. More like a kid's Happy Meal with a couple of small dry fish sandwiches and no tartar sauce

The fish and bread: The fish were most likely small and pickled, similar to sardines. And the bread was more like small dinner rolls. Since they were made with barley the family was probably poor as wealthy families used wheat when making bread.

The crowd: Scripture refers to the number of people who were fed after Jesus blessed the food as five thousand. But that number did not include women and children. When eating in public in Jewish culture during Jesus' time men ate separately from the women and children. Scholars estimate He fed between ten and fifteen thousand.

The boy: We typically hear about the characters in this story as Jesus, the crowd, and the disciples. But we neglect one of the central characters—the boy. We don't know where he came from, his name or his age. Many scholars say he was probably between the ages of six and twelve. What we *do* know is he didn't have much to offer but literally gave everything he had.

This was one young boy in a crowd of thousands. No one thought he mattered and could make a difference.

What if...

I find myself playing the 'what if' game and wondering: what if that little boy had said 'no' when the guy approached him and shared that Jesus wanted his lunch?

He could have reacted with a negative attitude as partially described by Andrew Thurbush in the following hypothetical interview:

Interviewer: Would you please describe for us what it was like watching Jesus perform a miracle with your lunch?"

Young Boy: "Well, mom packed my lunch in my favorite lunch box, and I was walking around in this big crowd. These guys came out of nowhere and asked if Jesus could use my lunch to feed all the people. I didn't say anything to them, but I thought to myself, 'there's no way He's going to feed over 5,000 people with a couple of fish sticks and some bread."

"But I went ahead and gave it to them. I can't explain how He did it, but I saw the whole thing with my own eyes, and it was absolutely amazing! I mean it was the coolest thing I've ever seen and just blew my mind."

"So, I bought like 50 copies of the Bethsaida Daily News with my allowance money I had saved. Then I realized later they didn't even include my name in the story. Not one single time. Do you have any idea how hard it is to prove to my family and friends that I was part of one of the biggest miracles Jesus performed? Nobody believes me. Not even my best friends at school. Honestly, this whole thing has been a real bummer."

Thankfully, the story didn't happen that way. The boy unselfishly sacrificed his small lunch and Jesus used His supernatural, divine power to satisfy the people's physical needs while teaching them about spiritual food.

For us that means we're never lost in the crowd. *We all have something to offer that can be used–even if no one notices.*

Several Spiritual Reminders:

The boy never received the glory, only the Messiah did. But imagine how that boy really felt when he saw what Jesus did with what little he offered. And no matter how small and insignificant we may feel, God can use us and what we offer to miraculously turn ordinary into extraordinary.

Bloom where you're planted!

My mother worked full-time outside our home as long as I can remember. Her jobs, like sewing clothes at a textile mill or working in a cubicle in large offices, didn't draw any attention. But she believed she could make a positive difference for Christ no matter where she was.

She suffered from cancer her last five years. During that most challenging and painful season in her life, she shared a meaningful message at churches and other groups titled, *Bloom Where You Are Planted*.

Mom strongly believed we can be used by God whoever and wherever we are. One of the points of her message was when we put our life in God's hands, He can use us to bless others. She truly 'walked the walk' of 'bloom where you are planted'.

I fail so many times but strive to practice the message she shared that life will never be the same when we place everything we are and have in God's hands.

All your talents, hopes, and dreams can *'Bloom where you are planted'*!

Positive Points to Ponder
- Never stop believing and don't lose hope because miracles happen every day. The fact that God gave you another day to wake up and live is a miracle in itself.
- You never know–today could be your breakthrough day—the day your life changes forever. *Your setback may be a set up for a comeback!*

19

Staying Steady in Your Storms

18 minutes. That's all it took for my friend and me to leave work, drive to the marina, and launch his boat in hopes of catching the big one. We did it so many times I couldn't keep count.

He was an experienced fisherman, and I just went along for the ride, enjoying nature and hoping to get the fish to nibble every now and then.

One overcast day as we drove to the lake, he shared that the weather forecast didn't look good and there was a possibility of a storm. He wondered aloud if we should go. Of course, I knew better than the radar and replied that we'll keep our eyes on the clouds and if it looks like rain, it won't take us long to return to the marina. Wrong answer.

We had just coasted into a little cove and cast our line the first time. Suddenly a bolt of lightning lit up the sky brighter than July 4th fireworks followed by a huge explosion of thunder. Before we could put on our raingear, we were drenched by the downpour which seemed to come in buckets.

I don't know what experience you recall that created indescribable fear, but for me this is it. Crossing the lake in a brutal electrical storm with the wind blowing nonstop, pounded by hail and rain as thunder and lightning filled the sky. It was more than enough to encourage me to catch up on my prayer life.

Perhaps this is why the story of the disciples experiencing a fierce storm affects me in such a personal way.

Snapshot Picture of Scripture. (Mark 4:35-41)

To get away from the large crowd, Jesus told the disciples to cross to the other side of the lake. So, they took Him into their boat and started the trip.

Soon a furious storm quickly came up with hurricane-like winds blowing and waves so high they were breaking into their boat. The disciples were terrified because they thought their boat was going to sink.

But while all this was happening, Jesus was sleeping in the stern on a cushion. The disciples frantically woke Him, and while shouting, asked if He cared they were going to drown.

He got up and commanded the wind and waves to be quiet and still. The wind immediately died down and everything was completely calm. Jesus then turned to the disciples and asked them why they were afraid and still didn't have faith.

The disciples turned to each other and in shock and amazement asked, "Who is this? Even the wind and the waves obey Him!"

The calm before the storm.

The Sea of Galilee is considered a relatively small body of water. It's about 13 miles wide, seven miles across, and can be 150 feet deep. What makes it so dangerous is that mountains surround it and when the warm and cold air mix it can result in violent storms that can develop in minutes.

This had been a busy and stressful day for Jesus. He had heard the news that His cousin John the Baptizer had been killed, and He wanted to get away from the crowds and be alone. But He was so popular the crowds followed Him. He felt compassion for them and had spent the entire day healing and teaching several parables.

Why life's storms can be a good thing.

When you face storms, it doesn't mean you've done something wrong. You can be doing exactly what God wants you to do and still face the most severe challenges. It doesn't mean you're going in the wrong direction or being punished.

It can mean you're going through something important before you get to the place God wants you to be. Sometimes He wants us to stay in the storm longer than we want. ***Sometimes He chooses not to calm the storm that's raging right now because He wants to calm 'you'.***

When things are happening to us that are hurting us, we tend to ask, "Why me?" Be ready because His response may be, "Why not you? Who is it that you want Me to allow this to happen to instead of you?" Scripture says we should thank and praise Him during the storm.

Sometimes God doesn't change your situation because He is

trying to change your heart!

Focus on the powerful lyrics to, *I Will Praise You* in *This Storm*, written by Bernie Herms and John Mark Hall and recorded by *Casting Crowns*:

> And I'll praise You in this storm
> And I will lift my hands
> For You are who You are,
> No matter where I am
> And every tear I've cried
> You hold in Your hand
> You never left my side
> And though my heart is torn
> I will praise You in this storm

As I reflect on storms in my life, it seems that most things I've learned about God that really matter I learned through a storm or crisis. As a result of a storm of health challenges, grief, finances, relationships, disappointments, or unwise decisions I made. I didn't learn through promotions, possessions, or recognitions.

Not all storms come to disrupt your life. Sometimes they come to clear the path so we can see our destination more clearly. Ever notice how the air seems more refreshing and clearer after a storm?

We can learn life lessons from children.

Children can teach us how to keep rainy times in perspective. When it starts raining, most adults tend to think it's going to ruin our plans. But kids look at rain as a time for fun. It's all about our perspective.

One Sunday I was waiting for Lucy in our car after church service. It had rained all morning but had now cleared off, leaving huge puddles in the parking lot.

I watched a little boy walk across the parking lot and suddenly stop. As if he was thinking, "Wait a minute. I'm a kid and I just walked *around* a huge puddle. Kids don't walk *around* puddles."

He retraced his steps and didn't just walk through the puddle but got a running start and jumped right in the middle of it–splashing water all over his Sunday best outfit. He then proceeded to repeat this at least six to eight times–laughing and enjoying life in his own world.

That is, until his mother came out of church seeing his completely soaked clothes. He was immediately escorted to their car. As they drove away, I could see her pointing her finger at him as her lips were moving rapidly.

Even though she had just received a blessing in service, I'm fairly certain she was not saying, "I love you very much and when we get home, I will give you extra ice cream for lunch."

Again, it is all about our perspective of rain and storms in our life.

"I didn't see *that* coming."

One of the biggest challenges about challenging times is we usually can't predict when they will start or their severity. Most of the time they are as unexpected and unpredictable as the weather. Often, we think to ourselves, "I didn't see *that* coming."

We all want to arrive, but most of us don't want the hassle involved in taking the trip. God can't take us *to* the mountaintop without going *through* the valleys and storms. Our storms and valleys have a purpose. It may seem like Jesus is sleeping on a pillow and not there, but He is always with you.

When you come out of a storm, you won't be the same person who walked into it. Realize you can't control what's happening to you, but you can control how you respond to it.

The disciples didn't realize the storm was going to be used by Jesus to teach them some incredible things about Himself and themselves. Like us, **the storms can become our real classroom**.

When you're in the middle of a storm, that's exactly where God can teach you who He is and how you never have to fear what comes your way.

> If a sea couldn't stop Moses,
> If a wall couldn't stop Joshua,
> If a giant couldn't stop David,
> Then no storm can stop you
> when God is with you!

Positive Points to Ponder
- We want Jesus to hurry and calm the storm. But He wants us to find Him in the middle of it.
- To have God in our life doesn't mean smooth sailing in a boat with no storms. It means having a boat that no storm can sink!

20

Celebrate Laughter Through the Hereafter

A friend once told me he enjoyed coming to my house because someone was usually laughing about something. I never thought about it until he mentioned it. Of course everything wasn't funny, but it started with my dad's healthy sense of humor. He believed it kept life in perspective and helped people feel comfortable around others.

One of his favorite phrases of wisdom included, "A family that laughs and prays together usually stays together." There is truly a time and place for everything, but most of us miss opportunities to smile, laugh, and celebrate life.

Lucy and I began dating while attending the same high school, and when reminiscing about our first date, we still 'laugh about laughing'. I called her the next day to see if she had a good time and she replied, "I don't think I've ever laughed so much in all my life."

That wasn't the response I anticipated, but since we have celebrated our Golden Wedding Anniversary, I'll consider it a compliment.

I've been asked if I think Jesus laughed and had fun. My answer is always a resounding "Yes. Absolutely!" One of the happiest events in our lives is attending weddings. The story when He was invited to a wedding has a joyful, surprise ending.

Snapshot Picture of Scripture. (John 2:1-11)

Jesus, His disciples, and mother were invited to a wedding. During the celebration, His mother, Mary, told Him the groom's family ran out of wine.

There were six 20-gallon stone water jars sitting nearby. Jesus told the servants to fill them with water. Then He told them to pour out a sample and take it to the master of ceremonies. When the host tasted it, the water had miraculously been turned into wine!

Not just any ordinary wine. He shared with the groom that everyone usually brings out the choice wine first, but this was special because they had saved the best wine until last.

This was the first sign or miracle recorded revealing Jesus' supernatural power and that He was the Messiah, and the disciples believed in Him.

It's party time—enjoy the feast, laugh, and dance the night away!

Many read this passage of scripture focusing mainly on the miracle itself. But it is imperative we understand some of the traditions and symbolism of a Jewish wedding feast during Jesus' day.

Wedding celebrations typically extended five to seven days. Autumn was the best time for marriage because the harvest was in, and the vintage was over. The groom was usually around twenty years old and the bride in her teens. The ceremony was attended by a small, select group of close friends and family members. But the entire village would be invited to the wedding feast.

Instead of the bride and groom going on a honeymoon, they stayed in town for the week-long celebration—enjoying the dancing, singing, laughter, food and wine with family and friends. It was truly a great time of joyful celebration!

Wedding receptions have changed for the better through the years. Receptions like those of our sons Jon and Chris and their wives, Angelee and Morgann give me an idea of what the wedding feast was possibly like. It included a fully catered meal and dancing to a live band or DJ—a real celebration!

Quite different from traditional receptions back in the day. They usually consisted of a table with bowls of peanuts, mints, and fruit punch. And the live music might be someone playing the hymn *I Surrender All* on a piano in the corner of the fellowship hall.

At just the right time—He turned the water into wine.

Hearing some people describe this special occasion, I get the impression they think after Jesus turned the water into wine, He found a quiet corner, took out some Hebrew manuscripts or scrolls, and read scripture to His disciples while everyone else was celebrating.

As believers, this is partly on us. We spend an abundance of time describing the divinity of Christ, but it's a little out of balance with how little we focus on His humanity. It's not wrong, just not the complete picture.

Jesus became very popular and was on the guest list of many weddings and meals in people's homes. Not just because of His healing and teaching, but He was a fun person to be around.

He was criticized often by the Pharisees and religious leaders for eating and drinking with nonbelievers. He broke all barriers—socioeconomic, religious, and racial.

They wouldn't have invited Him if He was known as a solemn, sad guy. I am not sure how you feel, but I don't like to hang out with boring people who rarely laugh and are not fun to be around.

Jesus himself said, "The Son of Man came eating and drinking, and you say, 'here is a glutton and a drunkard, a friend of tax collectors and sinners.'" (Luke 7:34 NIV)

I like the way Jesus is described by the staff and author Max Lucado in the book *He Gets Us*. They share that one of the reasons people were drawn to Jesus was not just a result of His miracles, but He connected with them.

We sometimes forget Jesus didn't go to the wedding at Cana to perform a miracle. He made that decision after He arrived, (with a strong suggestion from His mother). He went because He was invited and looking forward to having a good time with friends. Almost sounds too simple, doesn't it?

And the wine. Scholars share that research shows the grapes grown in that area produced a very dark red wine. So, when Jesus told His disciples at the Last Supper to drink the wine 'for this is the blood of My covenant,' that may be one of the few things they actually understood.

Since the beginning of the Bible, people considered wine to be a gift from God because it represents joy in the Lord. (Deuteronomy 14:26 and Psalm 4:7) So, when Jesus changed the water into wine, it was more than just a beverage to go with the food. Understanding the Mid Eastern culture helps us understand how it played a central part of the wedding and had a special meaning for the bride, groom, and their guests.

Holy Humor and The Laughing Christ.

In 1973 Willis Wheatley sketched a picture of Jesus and titled it *The Laughing Christ*. I absolutely love the picture as it most closely describes a human emotion of Jesus we rarely think about or see—laughter.

With a brief search you can instantly see the picture demonstrating His humanity I have attempted to portray. His head is tilted back, and His mouth open with a side-splitting laugh, as if someone at the wedding has just shared a hilarious story with Him. *Laughter through the hereafter.*

Laughter sometimes begins with a smile, and children's honesty makes my day. I recall a television show on which the host interviewed children and their honest answers were great examples of healthy humor.

He asked a little girl once what her favorite Bible story was. He was surprised when she quickly responded that it was the one when Jesus changed the water into wine.

Her reason was even better. He asked what she thought the story meant, and she quickly replied, "I'm not sure but I guess it means when you run out of wine, you better get on your knees and pray."

Years ago I served as the Youth Director of a church and presented a program to the congregations titled, "Holy Humor." I shared that as Christians we should follow the examples found in Scripture demonstrating the joyful message of Christ through our smiles, laughter, and a healthy sense of humor.

I shared familiar stories such as Sarah, who at the age of about 90 became pregnant by Abraham, who was around 100. She had an unforgettable response. She said that God had brought her laughter, and everyone who hears about what happened will laugh with her.

Sometimes God uses everyday situations to make us briefly pause in our busyness and smile. Recently I saw a sign in someone's yard that made me smile:

No Soliciting
We are too broke to buy anything
We know who we are voting for
We have already found Jesus
Seriously, unless you are selling Thin Mints
Please go away and have a blessed day!

More to the miracle than turning water into wine.
Jesus will provide for all your needs. In this story He showed compassion for the family by providing wine. He does the same for each of us on a daily basis. You don't have to be concerned about

finances, food, physical needs, or the future because He will take care of you.

God sometimes saves the best for last. Reflecting on the wedding, if they hadn't run out of the good wine they wouldn't have tasted the best. When you think you are running out of resources or opportunities and have nothing left, remember that is the time God shows up.

When you feel like it's the end with nothing to laugh about and nothing to celebrate, He will step in and say, "I have saved the best for now."

Instead of focusing on the wine, focus on the Winemaker. We need to understand and appreciate this amazing miracle or sign. But it is more important to focus and put our complete trust in the One who not only has the supernatural power to change the chemical composition of a liquid, but can transform our lives.

Christ is the only person who can bring true joy and life-long laughter every day. Now *that* is something to celebrate!

Positive Points to Ponder
- The same person who changed water into wine can change you, your life, and your future!
- Jesus changed water into wine. Imagine what He can do with *You*!

21

Radical Religion or Remarkable Relationship?

When I shared with someone during my younger days that I was a PK (pastor's kid), people showed interesting reactions. Many were similar to Lucy's parents when we started dating. Like most parents they asked what my father did for a living.

She replied that dad was a pastor, and they responded with the typical forced smile and a cordial, "Oh, that's nice." (Possibly thinking, 'I've heard about those PK's and hope this relationship doesn't get too serious'.)

With all the mandatory church attendance, you would think our reputation would be more positive. We didn't hold a family meeting on Sunday mornings to vote on whether Ronda and I would attend church. It was understood if the church doors were open, we would be there.

From the first grade, when my dad entered seminary, until I left home for college I had almost perfect attendance. That means attending on: Sunday morning for Sunday School and Worship Service, Sunday evening for youth group meeting and worship service, and Wednesday evening for Bible Study.

I emphasize the word *almost* perfect attendance because it was a rarity to miss church. I clearly recall one specific occasion.

The second Sunday of February 1964 I faked a stomach-ache so I could stay home and watch a television program. Not just *any* program, but the Beatles made their highly anticipated appearance on the Ed Sullivan Show. Everyone at school would be talking about it, and I was determined not to miss it.

I was one of seventy-three million Americans to watch them sing several songs in front of many screaming, swooning fans. They opened with *All My Loving* and closed with *I Want to Hold Your Hand*–which became their best-selling single. (I later confessed to my parents that I skipped church, and to my surprise they understood.)

So, what about church attendance? Does the Bible and Jesus specifically address the subject? Is it really *that* important? You may never have attended church, attended but quit and have no intention of returning, been an active participant most of your life or fall somewhere in between.

Wherever you are on the spectrum, I trust you will discover some helpful, interesting, and possibly surprising insights about church attendance. Let's take a brief look at how this entire 'church thing' started.

Snapshot Picture of Scripture (Acts 2:42-47)

After Christ's resurrection and ascension, His followers started meeting together in homes and temple courts. They gathered to fellowship, listen to the apostles' teaching, break bread, pray, and praise.

Everyone was amazed the apostles were performing signs and miracles just like Jesus did! Some followers were so committed, they sold their property and gave the proceeds to support the ministry and the needs of others. As a result, many new people were becoming a part of the church every day.

The early church was about people—not a building.

A reminder that the book in the New Testament we commonly refer to simply as Acts is titled the Acts of the Apostles. It is one of the most reliable books regarding the history of the early Christian church.

Ten days after Christ ascended—50 days after the resurrection—the Holy Spirit visited the place where the believers were gathered and experienced Pentecost. This is considered by most scholars as the birthday or beginning of the Christian church.

Later they began meeting in different places. So instead of thinking of the church as a building, think about a body or community of believers.

Attending Church: Why some people do or don't—will or won't.

Statistics show that less people in America are attending church than before the pandemic. According to a 2023 Gallup Poll church attendance levels are about 10% less than 10 years ago.

Numerous reasons or excuses shared for not attending include: too busy, tried it and didn't get anything out of it, find spiritual fulfillment in other ways, since the pandemic just never returned, and churches are full of hypocrites.

The overwhelming reason most often given for nonattendance is because Christians are hypocrites. It is important to address this issue because it is *true*! Say what? That's correct. We Christians are all hypocrites and that's just one of our many faults.

The church is made up of imperfect, spiritually sick people like *me*, who make mistakes and are messed up. The Church is meant to be a hospital for us sick folk and not a country club for saints.

There is only one perfect person who physically lived on earth. Breaking News—it isn't you and I can assure you it isn't me.

We are all spiritually sick and need healing. Jesus said, "It is not the healthy who need a doctor, but the sick" (Mark 2:17 NIV). I've always had trouble understanding why some people think Christians who attend church are supposed to be perfect. **One of the reasons we attend is because we admit we are broken and need to be repaired.**

Expecting people at church to be spiritually perfect would be like me joining a fitness facility and as I look around, I see that many of the members are overweight, and some are more out of shape than me. So, I made the decision not to return.

Sadly, they are overlooking the members who were very unhealthy and out of shape when they first joined. But through hard work and a commitment to regular visits are now much healthier.

And I respectfully share with folk who say they tried church but were disappointed, so they never returned. I enjoy going out to eat at restaurants. But if I tried a place and received terrible service and food, I assure you I may not visit that specific business again, but I would never stop eating out at restaurants.

So, who is the church for? The spiritually fit who have been a believer for years, nonbelievers who haven't started their faith journey, or folk who started but wandered away? Actually, **the beauty of the church is that it is for everyone. There's plenty of room at the table.**

GOOD NEWS YOU CAN USE

Hypocrites in Heaven

I was shocked, confused, and bewildered, as I entered heaven's door;
Not by the beauty of it all, or the pretty, golden decor.

But it was the folks in heaven, who made me sputter and gasp;
The thieves, liars and sinners, the hypocrites and other trash.

There's the kid from seventh grade, who stole my lunch money twice,
Next to him was my old neighbor, who never said anything nice.

I nudged Jesus, "What's the deal? I would love to hear Your take;
How'd all these sinners get up here, God must have made a mistake.

And why is everyone so quiet, so somber, give me a clue;
He said, "Quiet my child, they're all in shock. They never thought they would be seeing *you*!"

The other side of the coin.

In a 2023 survey people who attended church on a regular basis shared some of their reasons: "I need a regular connection and relationships with people who care about each other." "My life is full of problems and challenges, and I need encouragement." "It's a great place to learn how to live like Christ wants me to live." "Jesus tells us in the Word that we are to be a part of His church." "It gives meaning to my life."

Not only is Christ the founder of the church but He is also the foundation of the church–the Rock. Jesus told Simon Peter, "On this rock I will build my church" (Matthew 16:18 ESV).

Again, the church is not about a building but the people in the building. I remember as a kid forming an inverted hand clasp with fingers intertwined. Then saying, "This is the church, and this is the steeple, open the door and there's all the people."

A friend once shared that going to church doesn't make you a Christian any more than going to a fast-food restaurant makes you a cheeseburger. He added that missing church is missing out on God's blessings–beginning with fellowshipping with other imperfect people.

If you are an active part of a local church, you've discovered many of these truths, and I encourage you to continue doing so to receive

God's amazing blessings for your life.

Radical Religion or Remarkable Relationship?

Author, philosopher, and former atheist who converted to Christianity, C. S. Lewis shares the experience of walking in a room during an in-depth theological discussion and being asked what makes Christianity different from other religions.

He responded that there is an easy answer. It's because of *grace*–unearned favor of God. It's a free gift that can't be bought or earned. All the other religions are spelled–DO. What can we do for someone to please them or reach a higher level of spirituality?

Christianity is spelled–DONE. Christ already did everything for us on the cross. There's nothing else for us to do. When we put our faith in Him, we are His child. **It's not about religion, it's about a relationship!**

Perhaps you need to reestablish the habit of regular participation in church. Pray as you begin your 'church search' and look for one that teaches and preaches the truth of the Bible. Don't be concerned if it doesn't have a $100,000 dollar laser light show during worship or if the pastor doesn't look like a GQ model.

If you've tried church and instead of joy it left you with guilt and disappointment, you found religion–not a relationship. Some people don't get this whole 'Jesus thing' because they had a negative experience with religious people. I get that but here's the thing. *People* will let you down, disappoint you and sometimes desert you. But Jesus won't–ever!

The church will never be perfect because it's full of messed up people like me and you. But it's a great place to learn how to love others because God loves everyone. And like the father of the prodigal son, our Heavenly Father will welcome you back home with open arms. In fact, He is pursuing you when you take a detour.

We all have times when we feel far from God. Some of us walked away while others of us drifted without realizing it. How we got there doesn't matter. What matters is what we do next. A step toward God and His church is a step toward the home you've been looking for. Just like the people in it, it's not perfect. But it is true, **'there's no place like home'!**

Positive Points to Ponder
- Church is not something we just *go to*. It's an amazing family we *belong* to.
- The difference between Jesus and religion:
  Religion shames people for having dirty feet. Jesus kneels and washes them.

22

Be a Dream Maker–Not a Heartbreaker

After an unusually busy, stressful season in our lives, Lucy and I reserved a lakefront cabin for a much-needed get-away weekend. The first night we were awakened about 4:00 a.m. by the sound of someone yelling, "You can do this. Pull, pull, pull. You're almost there!"

Rubbing the sleep from my eyes, I squinted out the window just in time to see a college rowing team practicing for a competition. A person was sitting in the front of the boat with a portable bullhorn yelling encouraging words to his tired, exhausted team members. (After watching the phenomenal movie, *The Boys In the Boat,* years later I learned the 'encourager' is officially called the cox'n.)

As a result of hearing the encouragement, I got excited about a sport that I knew absolutely nothing about. My adrenaline started flowing, and my eyes were fixated on watching the boat skim across the moonlit lake until they rowed out of sight.

There is a man mentioned in the New Testament named Barnabas who was known to be an encourager.

Snapshot Picture of Scripture (Acts 4:36-37; 9:26-28; 11:21-24)

The first passage gives us several key facts about Barnabas. His name was actually Joseph, but the apostles nicknamed him Barnabas which means 'son of encouragement'. He was a Levite, one of the most important tribes in Israel. They were responsible for the religious leadership of the Jews and provided services in the temple.

Like many believers in the early church, Barnabas sold some of his property and used the proceeds to support the apostles' ministry.

The apostle Paul had a horrible reputation before he became a believer. The original apostles were scared of him and wouldn't accept him as a disciple.

But Barnabus told them about Saul's conversion and how he had heard him preach boldly in Damascus. So, they finally allowed Saul to stay with them, and he began preaching in Jerusalem.

The church in Jerusalem heard the exciting news about large numbers of people becoming believers in Antioch. So, they sent Barnabas there, and when he arrived, he encouraged them to stay true to the Lord and keep up the ministry of spreading the Good News.

Build a bridge or break a blessing.

If Barnabas hadn't been the bridge between Paul and the disciples, they most likely would not have accepted him to be part of the ministry. Think about that. Barnabas was the key influencer and encourager to the disciples, and yet many people know very little about him.

Some scholars say that if Barnabas hadn't convinced the apostles to accept Paul as a partner in their ministry, almost half of the New Testament would be missing!

Be careful of the applause.

Many times encouragers go unnoticed. They are like the stage crew or support staff who work behind the scenes. Barnabas was making a major impact on the Christian movement and starting early churches himself. But like John the Baptist when Jesus entered the scene, Barnabas was willing to give up the star, main-man role and become a supporter and encourager to Paul.

It takes a heavy dose of humility to do that. Many times, it is necessary to swallow our pride. As leaders we must be careful that the attention and recognition don't go to our heads and instead choke down a hefty helping of healthy humble pie. And Jesus has the best recipe.

I recall the story of a young boy in elementary school who told his mother before leaving home one morning that he would be trying out for a part in the school play that day.

He came home that afternoon excitedly telling his mom he got a part in the play. She asked him what part he would be playing, and he explained, "The teacher wants me and a few others to play the important part of *encouragers*."

When she inquired exactly what he would be doing, he enthusiastically replied, "We get to sit in the front row with the audience and smile, clap, and encourage the other students on the stage."

Notice the phrase *get to*. He was so innocently humble he considered it a special privilege to support and encourage others. The life lessons we can learn from young people never cease to amaze me.

Words and small actions can make a BIG impact.

We may think the small things we say or do don't matter. But experience tells a different story. Scripture shares that we are given various gifts, including but not limited to, teaching, administrating, and *encouraging people.*

Regardless of which specific gift you may have, everyone is commanded to encourage others. "Therefore, encourage one another and build each other up, just as in fact you are doing" (1 Thessalonians 5:11 NIV).

True Story of An Encourager: I'm reminded of the story about Jamie, a man born with Down Syndrome. Finding employment was a challenge, but his father knew someone who owned a local grocery store and helped him get a job as a bagboy. It was not a very glamorous job, but he appreciated the opportunity and was determined to be the best bagboy in town.

It didn't take long for him to notice that not only were most of his customers in too much of a hurry to speak, but many of them looked stressed out and sad. So, he came up with an idea.

He asked his father to help him run off encouraging positive quotes on their computer, and Jamie carefully cut them into small strips of paper. He started putting a quote in customers' grocery bags hoping his words of encouragement would somehow brighten their day.

And did they ever! When customers approached the checkout area, they would look for the register where Jamie was bagging and get in his line. In fact, it wasn't long before the manager had a real problem. Even if the other registers had no customers, they would still get in Jamie's line—which sometimes extended all the way to the back of the store! *Jamie's experiment proved we all need and appreciate encouragement.*

Have you ever received too much encouragement? A time when people were so positive and encouraging you just could not take any more? You had to pray and ask the Lord to please stop sending the encouragement?

A time when your cup of encouragement was so full and overflowing it was running off the edge of the table. I would guess that, like me, you can't recall such an experience ever happening in your life.

Tim Tebow, former college and NFL star, shared in his Christian testimony that he always wanted to be so successful that one of his early goals was to be recognized as the MVP–Most Valuable Player.

But as a Christian, and later the founder of the *Tim Tebow Foundation,* he came to understand what is really important: he recognized that everyone we meet every day has a need that we know nothing about. People are hurting physically, emotionally, or spiritually, and some are abused. So, we need to encourage and help them—especially those who can't help themselves because they are truly the MVP–*Most Vulnerable People.*

Barnabas and Jamie are real world examples that all of us can be encouragers. We may not have gifts or talents that people notice like speaking in public, playing sports, or performing music. But we can encourage people to have a blessed day, hold a door for someone, or simply smile. *Your words of encouragement and small acts of kindness can make a BIG impact on someone's day and possibly their life!*

Positive Points to Ponder

- God usually prefers to work through people like us rather than perform miracles so we will depend on each other for encouragement.
- Today will never come again.
  Be a blessing, be a friend.
  Encourage someone, take time to care.
  Just let them know that you are there!

23

Rejuvenating Rest: Be Still and Just Chill

Following a recent health examination by my family physician, he shared his diagnosis and added some additional complications that can result from my condition. As you read the negative side effects, can you guess the *cause* of what 30% of all American adults and myself are experiencing?

Risk for diabetes and heart disease, stroke, high blood pressure, memory issues, irritability, and stress. If you guessed *Insomnia or sleep deprivation* you are correct. We adults aren't getting enough sleep and simply need to rest!

We see and hear those words often, but they don't seem to resonate with us. When driving on the Interstate, I see Rest Stops and inside are Rest Rooms. It seems the medical recommendation for most illnesses is 'drink plenty of fluids and rest'. After a funeral someone is laid to rest, and then we hope they rest in peace (RIP).

The Guiness World Record was set in 1986 when a guy went 453 hours–that's 19 days, without any sleep! Judging from my personal experience when I don't get a good night's sleep, I can only imagine what kind of mood he may have been in.

One of the main causes of sleep deprivation is our lifestyle of *busyness*. We feel like there is too much to do and not enough time to get it all done. We are afraid we won't be able to complete our daily to-do list. We are not only tired, many of us are sick and tired of being tired.

Regretfully, if we decide to lighten our responsibility load, many times the first things to go are spiritual—prayer, reading the Word, or attending church. Someone shared that *it is inconsistent to become too busy to spend an hour or two a week with God and then expect Him to spend eternity with us!* Ouch–that one hurt.

It would be beneficial to check out what Jesus said and did regarding rest.

Snapshot Picture of Scripture (Matthew 11:28-30 NLT)

Then Jesus said, "Come to me all of you who are weary and carry heavy burdens, and I will give you rest. Take my yoke upon you. Let me teach you, because I am humble and gentle at heart, and you will find rest for your souls. For my yoke is easy to bear, and the burden I give you is light."

A *yoke* is a curved piece of wood that goes around the neck of large animals to keep them together. The purpose is so they can pull a heavier load than would be possible by themselves. The word was used to describe someone in submission, and it is also a metaphor in scripture for bondage.

The reason we can find rest by taking Christ's yoke is that his yoke is different. When the Law was imposed on humans, it did not bring liberty–it brought bondage. The Pharisees codified 613 Mosaic Laws by adding over 1,500 "fence laws" or prohibitions for the people to obey.

The people were burdened down by man-made legalistic rules that God never commanded. When Christ looked at a nation under such a heavy burden and told them He would give them rest, it was a life-changing invitation.

His love for us makes all our burdens light and His yoke is easy. Our son Chris and Daughter-in-law Morgann found an old antique yoke and hung it on a wall in their home as a daily reminder of this comforting truth.

Let's begin at the beginning.

When contemplating the importance of rest, it's a refreshing reminder that during God's creation, He worked for six days and then rested.

And how important was resting to Moses when he gave the Ten Commandments in Exodus 20? You might think some of the 'big ones' would have the longest explanation. Murder? Four words. Stealing? Four words. Adultery? Five words. But Keep the Sabbath Holy and REST? 105 words!

Feeling blue over flipping the Blue Laws. It's disappointing what was done with this important command to set aside a specific day to focus on God and rest. Growing up in Virginia, we observed Blue Laws until they were overturned in 1988. Until that time the only businesses allowed to be open on Sundays were drug stores, and customers could only purchase medicine.

Pause and reflect, or imagine what Sundays were or would be like today with no restaurants, department stores, malls, movie theaters, or gas stations open. You may be thinking that life would be miserable, but I can assure you there would be more opportunities to spend time with the people we love and yes, time for more rest.

I find the reasons offered by the court for overturning the laws extremely disappointing. "Prohibiting Sunday shopping is not needed because a day of rest is unnecessary. Sunday itself is not the day of church and family dinners it once was. People are just not resting on Sunday anymore."

We have a choice of blaming the government for us not getting adequate rest, or we can accept responsibility for our own lives. There are some health challenges of which we have no control. But many times, we receive but don't pay attention to the warning signs.

When the gas level in my car gets low, the gauge will indicate the situation. As a second warning, a light will appear on my dash. And if I choose to ignore that one, a lady—who apparently is hiding inside my speakers—will verbally tell me, "This is your last warning. You only have enough gas to drive five more miles."

We need rest to become God's best.

Some synonyms for rest are peace, ease, relaxation, slow down, or sleep. And when considering rest we are reminded of the **three kinds of time:**

Prime Time–When we do our best work. For me it's early morning.

Grind Time–There are situations when we have no choice. Something has to be done, and we grit our teeth and do it.

Unwind Time–Most folk need to improve on prioritizing daily downtime and scheduling extended days to get away. Jesus told the disciples, "Come away by yourselves to a secluded place and rest awhile" (Mark 6:31 NASB).

Experts state there are several types of rest.
- **Physical Rest**–Our body needs adequate sleep and rest. Fitness experts say our muscles grow and improve during times of rest–not while we are busy and actively weight training or exercising.
- **Mental/Emotional Rest**–When we stop forcing our brain to

work so hard and give it time to process. Without it our memory will not be utilized to its maximum.
- **Spiritual Rest**–We are spiritual beings. The real you is the person living on the inside. Our souls need rest, too. We enter into God's rest when we become believers. And it's with the heart or spirit that we believe–no matter what the trouble or turmoil is around us. Resting allows us to quiet ourselves before God. He created rest for our benefit. *Rest restores us.*

When we look at our world we can get distressed.
When we look at ourselves we can get depressed.
But when we look at Christ we can find rest!

Basics we must know–Something has to go.

Even Christ is into cutting things out. In John 15, Jesus taught about branches bearing fruit. Sometimes he prunes the branches when necessary. Decide what, or sometimes who, you need to let go of, or put down, because it's hindering your growth and not allowing you to rest.

I will suggest a huge one—*screens*! Decide and find a way to reduce your daily use of cell phones and computers. Start small. No one at our home brings their cell phone to the table for meals. I encourage you to try it. I promise you will begin having meaningful conversations again.

Remember that God will never leave you empty. He will replace anything you cut away. If He asks you to put something down or let go, He may want you to pick up something later that will be greater.

Always make time for the spiritual. Don't ever be too busy to do the things that are easy not to do. Basics of spiritual growth like regular prayer time, worship with others, and reading the Word should never be marked off your to-do list. Starting your day with our Creator always makes the rest of the day better.

Be still and chill–during the day and for an extended stay.

Making yourself take brief breath-prayers is very beneficial. With a little creativity it's possible, even with others around. If you just read that and thought 'it can't be done in my situation', you are correct. Convince yourself it can be done, and then create ways to take 'mental vacations' during your busy day.

And it's vital to plan extended time away to relax and be still. God told David the psalmist to be still and know that He is God. And then

David reminds us in Psalm 23, "He leads me beside still waters, He restores my soul".

Jesus spent a lot of His ministry time near the Sea of Galilee. There is something relaxing and restful near the water. We are blessed to live about fifteen minutes from nearby Claytor Lake and less than a half-mile ride to the New River.

Find a way to start your 'rest and relax plan' today!

Positive Points to Ponder

- Sleep is the golden chain that ties our body, heart, and soul together.
- Rest is the sweet sauce secret ingredient that makes life come alive.

Section 2: GAME PLAN!

Everyone planning to compete or perform should prepare by knowing the basics, practicing the right way, and developing a game plan. It's the same with living a life of meaning and significance. For believers it begins with gaining knowledge and following the teachings of Christ as recorded in the Holy Bible.

Regretfully, even though the average American home has four copies, less than 20 percent of Christians read it between times of attending church.

How familiar are we with Scripture? In a recent survey, 25 percent of 300,000 participants could not correctly answer the following questions:

- Where in the Holy Bible is the 23rd Psalm found?
- Where in the Holy Bible is John 3:16 found?

(And we wonder if we need to return to the basics.)

Whether the extent of your knowledge of the Bible is somewhere between zero and a scholarly hero, this next "Game Plan" section is for YOU! It includes life-changing lessons found in some of the most important and familiar scripture passages.

CAUTION! Sometimes familiarity can be a roadblock to learning. My hope is wherever you are on your faith journey and Bible knowledge, you will prayerfully read the following stories and lessons, asking God to show you new insights and truths you have never experienced.

Are you ready? LET'S GO!

24

More Than Just a Book-of-the-Month

I once heard a speaker ask a large audience at a Christian conference to raise their hand if they had read the Bible cover-to-cover at least one time. About five or six hands went up.

"Well," he continued, "Forget about the table of contents, the maps, the index and all the other information, how about just Genesis through Revelation?" Similar results. In a last effort he asked, "Okay, how many have read the four gospels?" A few additional hands were raised.

He then light-heartedly reminded the crowd that for a lot of people, when they get to heaven, it's going to be a little awkward and possibly embarrassing. He hypothetically shared that after they are welcomed at the gate, there may be some other people waiting.

Like Obadiah and Philemon may come up and ask, "What's the problem? You didn't like the books we wrote? And some folks are going to have a blank look on their face that says, "What book? You wrote a book in the Bible?"

And when you greet another guy and say, "Hey Jude" he may reply, "My book was only one chapter. In all the years you spent on earth you didn't have time to read 25 verses? Really?"

A little humor always helps drive home a point and this was well taken. Recent polls by the Ponce Foundation found that out of over 2 billion Christians in the world, less than 30% will ever read through the entire Bible. And about 82% of American Christians only read their Bibles on Sundays while in church.

In this chapter you will discover or be reminded why this amazing book, the Holy Bible, is the best-selling book of all time, is the most reliable account we have of God, and is a guide to teach us how to live a fulfilling, abundant life!

Snapshot Picture of Scripture (1 Timothy 3:14-17 NLT)

It's difficult to know or understand Jesus' teachings without being familiar with the contents of the book in which they are recorded. He began His ministry with a reading from scripture. He quoted it often, and whether we are believers or unbelievers, it is the best way to discover real truth.

Timothy, a partner with Paul, shares our main Scripture passage. "But you must remain faithful to the things you have been taught. You know they are true, for you know you can trust those who taught you. You have been taught the holy Scriptures from childhood, and they have given you the wisdom to receive the salvation that comes from trusting Christ Jesus. All Scripture is inspired by God and is useful to teach us what is true and to make us realize what is wrong in our lives. It corrects us when we are wrong and teaches us to do what is right."

Jesus asked an important question to the religious leaders. "Didn't you ever read this in the Scriptures? The stone that the builders rejected has now become the cornerstone" (Mark 12:10 NLT). Many times, the *cornerstone* refers to the foundation of a building. Reading and studying scripture is how we learn the basic instructions of how to live.

What if I told you...

What if I gave you a copy of the number one best-selling book of all time and told you its message has made millions of lives better and can do the same for you. Would you be at least a little interested in reading or hearing it?

There was a television show years ago, and when one of the detectives interviewed a suspect, he would always inform the person, "Just the facts, please. Just the facts." The facts we know about the Bible are almost beyond comprehension.

It is truly *the* book of books, which is what the word 'Bible' means. It has over 63,779 overt connections or cross references! That would be extremely impressive if it was written by one person. But in his book *52 Weeks Through the Bible*, James Merritt shares that it contains 66 books in one volume written by 40 different authors living on three different continents. And the authors wrote it in three different languages over a period of 1,500 years!

Despite all the diversity of people, time, geography, and languages there is a divine thread that connects all the books, and it tells one united story about God's love, grace, and forgiveness. In comparison, there is no other book in all human civilization that even scratches the surface as a close second.

It is by far the most read book in history. The whole Bible has been translated into 349 languages. Conservative statistics put the total number of Bibles sold at more than five billion.

It is a fascinating book, and how it comes together cannot be explained simply by assuming it is a coincidence. For example, many scholars agree that:

>Psalm 117 is the shortest chapter in the Bible
>Psalm 118 is the middle chapter of the Bible
>Psalm 119 is the longest chapter in the Bible

I would imagine there is a possibility the thought crossed your mind wondering 'if this book is so amazing, interesting, and life-changing, why don't more people read it'? Over five million people from across the United States were asked that specific question, and their top answers were similar to why most of *us* don't read it as often as we could or should.

Their top answers include: don't know where to begin, don't understand it, and don't see its relevance in their life. All are truthful and typical responses. If you ever thought one or more of those hang with me as I address them and share a few benefits or reasons of encouragement to begin, return, or keep digging deeper.

Real reasons to read.
1. **The unity of the biblical message.** As noted earlier, the circumstances surrounding the writing of the Bible would seem to guarantee its fallibility and yet its message is amazingly consistent.
2. **To know and understand the truth.** Counterfeit specialists look for things like ink, paper, and serial numbers to know what is real. If people aren't familiar with scripture, they won't be able to tell the difference between counterfeit doctrine and real truth.
3. **The positive impact it has on people's lives.** Perhaps one of the most important reasons is that the Bible has changed the lives of millions of people all over the world. It is not about what we can do to earn the favor of God. It is about having a personal relationship with Him.
4. **We can trust its accuracy and reliability.** The *Dead Sea Scrolls*

discovered in 1947 are astonishingly similar to the Hebrew Bible. Additionally, in 2023 the *Codex Sassoon* was sold for over 38 million dollars. It was verified by Sothby's to be the oldest handwritten manuscript over one thousand years ago on 792 pages of sheepskin and includes all 24 books of the original Hebrew Bible, missing only 8 pages!

5. **An unfathomable number of prophecies made hundreds of years ago have been fulfilled.** What are the odds that 360 Messianic prophecies about Jesus would happen? Peter Stoner, an authority on probability, shared that the odds of one man fulfilling eight prophecies is 1 in 100 quadrillion (10 to the 17th).

To put that probability in perspective, that would be like covering the entire state of Texas with silver dollars 2 feet deep, marking one of them and burying it. Then randomly a blindfolded person lands by helicopter, walks as far as they wish, reaches down, and pulls out the marked silver dollar. That would be the odds of one man fulfilling 8 prophecies. *Jesus fulfilled 360!*

The Bible is more easily accessible than ever.

I wonder what would happen if we treated our Bibles like we treat our cell phones. I recall a credit card advertisement years ago with the slogan, "Don't leave home without it." Most of us never leave home without our phones. What if we never left home without our Bibles? And if we did forget it, what if we immediately returned home so we could have it with us?

What if when we have an emergency, we turn to the Bible first instead of a last resort? What if when we lost our way in life and didn't know how to get home, we used it as our spiritual GPS? And what if we checked it for messages when we wake up and during the day as often as we check our phones? After all, *God always has a helpful and encouraging message for us!*

The exciting news is, as a result of amazing technology, we *can* have the Bible with us most of the time—on our cell phones. There is something special about holding a physical copy of the Bible. But when that's not practical or possible we can have access to an electronic copy.

I have shared what Scripture says about the importance of reading the Word, some facts about this phenomenal book, and why we should read it. But one of my most important purposes is to offer a simple reading plan you can begin *today*.

- To help understand what you're reading, utilize the internet to search for *an easy-to-understand translation of the Holy Bible*. Then download one of the translations available. Some are free. (If you are not a reader, utilize the audio version.) People have different opinions regarding which translation is best, but doing this is a huge first step toward reading the Word more consistently.
- There are multiple recommendations on *where to start or restart,* but some of the most common include: 1) The four gospels—the life, teachings and ministry of Christ, 2) Ephesians—to know how to live a Christian life, 3) James—to learn how to apply Scripture to your life, 4) Proverbs—how to live life well, and 5) Psalms—sharing your emotions with God.

Like most people, I have personally experienced dry-bone periods of my life and not read the scriptures as I should. When I returned, it was like putting cables on my spiritual battery and jump-starting it with new energy and meaning.

The Bible resonates with truth in the deepest part of the human soul. It is the foundation on which we can all build our lives!

Positive Points to Ponder
- Many books can inform you, but there is only one that can transform you forever!
- The Bible was meant to be bread for daily use—not cake for special occasions.

Important Note: If you are interested in personally 'digging deeper' or want to use this book as a guide for a small group study, please turn to the Study Guide on page 180.

25

A Reason for Every Season

Recently I was asked which of the four seasons was my favorite and why. It is a simple question but not as easy to answer as I originally thought.

My first inclination was to say 'fall'. We live in the southern part of Virginia and when the leaves change into a collage of colors—orange, yellow, and red—it's simply God's paintbrush of creation. Additionally, it's football season. High school Friday Night Lights and Saturday's noon-to-midnight marathon of college games.

After additional consideration and recalling past memories, the choice became more difficult. Winter means building a snowman, sledding, and schools being closed for 'snow days'. Spring means fresh green grass, flowers and getting outside. And summer brings back memories of fun-filled family vacations at the beach and more time at the river or lake.

Since it is a multiple-choice question, I will take the easy way out and check E—All of the above. What's your favorite season and why?

Part of God's great design of the earth is seasons. Wet and dry, hot and cold, and since both my grandfathers were farmers, I'll include planting and harvesting. We find in the scriptures that our lives also experience seasons.

The common Christian English translations follow the Septuagint in placing the order of King Solomon's three books as: Proverbs, Ecclesiastes, then the Song of Solomon. Let's look at one of the most familiar passages of his writings.

Snapshot Picture of Scripture (Ecclesiastes 3:1-8 NLT)

1. For everything there is a season, a time for every activity under heaven.
2. A time to be born and a time to die. A time to plant and a time to harvest.

3. A time to kill and a time to heal. A time to tear down and a time to build up.

4. A time to cry and a time to laugh. A time to grieve and a time to dance.

5. A time to scatter stones and a time to gather stones. A time to embrace and a time to turn away.

6. A time to search and a time to quit searching. A time to keep and a time to throw away.

7. A time to tear and a time to mend. A time to be quiet and a time to speak.

8. A time to love and a time to hate. A time for war and a time for peace.

In these verses Solomon presents a list of 14 contrasting seasons and times. Together these pairings communicate a sense of every human activity in its different forms. While appearing to be opposites, each pair is more like a counterpart–both having their appropriate place.

Through these comparative statements, he is simply saying that God is always working out His good purposes and accomplishing His will in each moment of our lives. (Romans 8:28)

The meaning doesn't need to be a mystery.

As we contemplate the meaning of this passage, I'm reminded of the story about the teacher who gave her class a special assignment. She instructed her students to list what they personally considered to be the seven wonders of the world.

When the students shared their lists, some of the most frequent answers included: the Empire State Building, the Egyptian Pyramids, the Grand Canyon, and China's Great Wall.

But one student hadn't finished and explained to the teacher that she was having trouble completing her list. The teacher asked her to share what she had written so far.

She began reading, "To me, the wonders of the world are God's gifts; to see, to touch, to hear, to laugh and to love." The entire classroom became deadly silent. No one said a word–including the teacher.

This young girl had learned at an early age what Solomon was sharing in this passage during his later years. While looking for the extraordinary, we sometimes take for granted the ordinary seasons, senses, or emotions we experience. In verse four he shared *a time to cry, laugh, mourn, and dance.*

When reading Ecclesiastes, it's obvious Solomon had experienced the highs and lows of life and was trying to make sense of it. He wondered, reflected, and asked questions similar to ones many of us ask: Why is there so much suffering? Where is God in the midst of all our challenges? What is my purpose for being here?

As pointed out by author Pamela Palmer, in this third chapter we find some clarity around these mysteries of life. When nothing seems to make sense, if we find God's presence in life, that's when real meaning and satisfaction will emerge. Life without God is hopeless and has no eternal meaning. But a life lived for God is one marked by fullness and significance.

As we know, life can be hard. Seemingly bad things happen to everyone, including followers of Christ. We know that each of us will experience difficult seasons as often as joyful seasons. And our seasons aren't like an egg timer. We don't know when they will begin or end.

I'm reminded that David was seventeen years old when the prophet Samuel anointed him to become the next King of Israel. But before he became King, David went back to work in the fields for the next thirteen years as a shepherd. He had to go through a long season of waiting. In other words, **he was anointed but not yet appointed**. Perhaps I'm not the only person for whom waiting seasons are some of my most challenging times.

Never Judge Someone Based On A Season

One season David was a shepherd, the next season he was a king. One season Ruth was working in the field, the next season she owned the same field. *We serve a God who turns things around in a season and this one may be yours!*

What we can learn while life continues to churn.

Our Heavenly Father is in total control of all things—including our seasons. Read verse one again, as it is a summary of the other seven. He is with us during life's toughest battles. He guides us from one season to the next.

Our greatest hope in seasons of despair is that God will never leave us there. We may think we won't make it, but His timing is always on time, every time, at just the right time.

Whatever season you are experiencing is not by accident. Every season has a purpose and can bring you into a closer relationship with God and create an unshakable faith. (James 4:8) God brings us to new seasons, changes our circumstances, and adds new meaning to our lives. *He can help you make sense of every season and cause your life to be abundant in meaning!*

Positive Points to Ponder
- *A season of transformation*: Grapes must be crushed to make juice or wine. Diamonds must be formed under pressure. Olives must be pressed to release oil. If you are in a season of transformation…trust God's process!
- There is a reason a windshield is larger than the rear-view mirror. Your future is more important than your past. God is ready to create a new season in your life–beginning today!

26

God's Top Ten
Is the Perfect Place to Begin

Most folk have done more than our fair share of complaining about laws we don't like to follow but have no choice. And it doesn't take long to find how seemingly absurd some of them are. Below are several that appear a little crazy and, in some cases, ridiculous. (The names of the states have been omitted to eliminate any potential embarrassment to the fine citizens who live there.)

In at least one state it is illegal to…
- sell pickles unless they bounce when dropped from a height of one foot.
- eat fried chicken with anything other than your hands. (Known as the 'Finger Lickin' Chicken Law'.)
- throw snowballs or other missiles at people.
- set a limit on the size of a personal beverage container. (Known as the 'Big Gulp Law'.)
- throw litter out of an aircraft while it is flying.

The prohibitions above are absolutely for real, on-the-books laws, and as folks say, "You can't make this stuff up." Many laws are intended for our protection and safety.

Can you imagine what driving would be like without speed limits? From interstates to areas around schools, to your neighborhood. They would not be anyone's safe place.

The Ten Commandments are also for our safety and protection, serve as God's holy standards for living in a covenant relationship, and give us basic rules of behavior for spiritual and moral living.

Snapshot Picture of Scripture (Exodus 20:1-17)
While Moses was on top of Mt. Sinai receiving the Ten

Commandments from God, the people became impatient. So, they made and started worshiping an altar in the shape of a golden calf.

When Moses came down the mountain carrying the tablets and saw what they were doing, he became so filled with anger he threw down the tablets and smashed them to pieces.

At God's command Moses later chiseled two new stone tablets just like the originals. These tablets became one of the items the Israelites carried in the Ark of the Covenant.

After reading the Ten Commandments in the above scripture, it's understandable how people can view them as a list of 'negative do's, don'ts, and thou shalt nots'. Below are examples of a paraphrase–not a translation or transliteration–stated in a positive manner.

1. Love God more than anyone else and make Him the first priority in your life.
2. Worship only YAHWEH–the one true God.
3. Say and use God's name with love and respect.
4. Keep the Sabbath day Holy and make time to rest.
5. Honor and be respectful to your parents.
6. Respect the dignity of every human life.
7. Be faithful to your husband or wife.
8. Only take things that belong to you.
9. Be truthful in everything you say and do.
10. Be content, satisfied, and grateful for all that God has given you.

Amazing History! One of the earliest known copies of the Ten Commandments was written in soot on a strip of goatskin found in the late 1940's among the Dead Sea Scrolls. The scrolls were written by scribes belonging to a collective of celibate Jews from the sect known as the Essenes. The documents had rested, undisturbed and preserved for two thousand years in darkness and dry desert air.

They are the foundation of all law in the Bible and are one of the most famous pieces of religious literature in the world.

It is interesting that the original manuscripts of the Bible never actually calls or refers to these ten laws Moses shared as the 'Ten Commandments'. The Hebrew expression means "ten words". Actually, they didn't play an important part in Christianity until the thirteenth century when they were used in church catechisms to instruct the youth.

Reflecting on my youth, the first time I remember hearing about the Ten Commandments was in early elementary school while attending Vacation Bible School. I recall the situation because our teacher challenged us that anyone who memorized and recited them for the class would get two candy bars as a reward. Having a serious sweet tooth, I accepted her challenge and enjoyed every bite of my Mounds and Almond Joy.

Are the Ten Commandments relative to our lives today?

Absolutely—YES! When Jesus, the Master Teacher, had just finished teaching the Beatitudes to the huge crowd of followers during the Sermon on the Mount, He addressed this very question. "Do not think I have come to abolish the Law or the Prophets; I have come not to abolish them but to fulfill them" (Matthew 5:17 NIV).

One of the differences between the old and new covenant can be found in Hebrews 8:10 NIV, "I will put my laws in their minds and write them on their hearts." Now that Christ had arrived, the heart and mind were more important than the stone tablets.

As new creatures in Christ, the law should not be a duty but a delight. If we want to love Christ as He deserves, we should strive to keep His commands.

Pharisees' phoniness is almost funny.

It must have been almost entertaining to the disciples when the Pharisees asked Jesus trick questions to test Him knowing His unexpected answers were going to be completely beyond their comprehension.

Scripture says people were astonished at His teaching. Matthew records an encounter when one of them asked Jesus which of the commandments is the greatest. Possibly expecting Him to name one of the Top Ten—like murder, adultery, or maybe stealing.

I can see the disciples winking at each other as if to say, "Uh oh, they better get ready because here it comes. They should know by now they can't stump Him."

Jesus quickly responded by saying, "Love the Lord your God with all your heart, and with all your soul, and with all your mind. This is the first and greatest commandment. A second is equally important. Love your neighbor as yourself" (Matthew 22:36-40 NLT).

I visualize the Pharisees standing there completely dumbfounded by His answer, not knowing what to say as Jesus calmly "dropped the mic" and walked away.

Important: What is so amazing about His answer is Jesus just condensed the Top Ten into the Terrific Two. *Upon review of the original Ten Laws, numbers one through four focus on loving God and numbers five through ten focus on loving others!*

The Top Ten and the Terrific Two have *everything* to do with the Good News!
1. The fact that we have these divinely delivered guidelines on how to enjoy and live the fullest life possible is Good News!
2. The Ten Commandments lead us to discover the Good News!
3. Since God sent His Spirit to transform us, one of the goals of the Ten Commandments is realized in the Good News!

Positive Points to Ponder
- It would be interesting to know what the Ten Commandments would look like if Moses had to get the approval of the U. S. Congress for them.
- Man has made over 40 million laws over the past 3,000 years—all of which are to enforce the Ten Commandments.

27

Shy Sheep Need a Sharp-Minded Shepherd

Like many children, my first introduction to sheep was reading a nursery rhyme that went something like, "Little Bo Peep lost her sheep and didn't know where to find them."

I always thought that was a sad situation for a young kid to read about. I mean this little girl lost her sheep, looked everywhere, and they are nowhere to be found. She probably had her family and everyone in the neighborhood involved in the search.

And of course there's the age-old advice for resting: "When you can't sleep, just count sheep." I tried that a few times, but it never worked. It usually led me to think about pork chops, and then I would get hungry which resulted in getting out of bed to fix a midnight snack.

My first real encounter with sheep was spending part of the summers on my grandparents' farm as a teen. I've never met a person who makes their living being a shepherd. But the closest person to it would be my Granddad Glenn. As a farmer, one of his many responsibilities was taking care of his flock of sheep.

I enjoyed lots of things while staying with my grandparents including Granny's home cooking, fishing in their pond, and especially going with Granddad when he herded the sheep from the field into the barn.

In the Old Testament we learn that David was a shepherd boy years before he became a king. He wrote many of the Psalms including Psalm 23. It is the most read, most well-known, and most memorized passage of scripture in the entire Bible. It is considered the universal Psalm, the chief Psalm, and the pearl of Psalms.

As with all the familiar passages of scripture, before reading or refamiliarizing yourself with it, prayerfully ask and expect God to show you new insights or remind you of ones forgotten and to open the eyes of your heart.

Snapshot Picture of Scripture. (Psalm 23:1-6 NKJV)
   1 The LORD is my shepherd; I shall not want.
   2 He makes me lie down in green pastures; He leads me beside the still waters.
   3 He restores my soul; He leads me in the paths of righteousness for His name's sake.
   4 Yea, though I walk through the valley of the shadow of death, I will fear no evil; for You are with me; Your rod and Your staff, they comfort me.
   5 You prepare a table before me in the presence of my enemies; You anoint my head with oil; my cup runs over.
   6 Surely goodness and mercy shall follow me all the days of my life; and I will dwell in the house of the LORD forever.

Exactly what's this shepherd and sheep thing all about?
   It can be a challenge for us to grasp the true meaning of these verses from David's perspective. So, let's put on our David glasses and read this passage while walking in his shoes—when and where he lived.
   The Shepherds: During the time of the Old Testament, it was often the youngest boy in the family. His main job was to protect the sheep day and night and make sure they were properly fed. During biblical times sheep were valuable to families in the Middle East as they relied upon them to provide wool, food, and clothes.
   Fast forward to the New Testament and we find that the shepherds near Bethlehem are the ones chosen to witness the heavenly announcement of Christ's birth. And Jesus refers to Himself as the Good Shepherd who truly cares for His sheep. (John 10:1-16)
   The Sheep: In the spring shepherds must constantly watch for 'cast sheep'. Because of heavy winter wool or being pregnant, they can easily slip or fall onto their backs. When this happens they are completely helpless and need their shepherd to help them get on their feet.
   Then, to help them get their equilibrium back, the shepherd gently holds their faces in his hands, looks into their eyes, and lovingly assures them everything is going to be okay. *What a picture of love as our Good Shepherd does the same thing with us.*
   Let's take a brief trip through each of the six verses in this power-packed passage of Scripture while looking for life-lessons we can learn!

Breaking it down and lifting us up.

Read verse 1: Tells us that the shepherd meets the sheep's every need: food, water, rest, safety, and guidance. And with God he doesn't need anything else.

You're probably aware that sheep are not considered to be the smartest animals on the planet. Let me say it another way. You may have seen different animals like dogs, elephants, lions, or horses perform tricks at a circus or ball game. I doubt you will ever see sheep jumping through hoops, catching balls, or rolling over.

They simply don't know how to survive without help. I've seen my granddad bundle up and walk outside in all kinds of weather to make sure the sheep are safe and have plenty of water and food.

Read verse 2: Key words are the verbs *makes* and *leads*. If the shepherd didn't make them lie down, they wouldn't rest. And rather than drive them like cattle, sheep don't know where to go, so the shepherd leads them by walking in front.

Sheep are afraid of just about everything, especially moving water. There was a small creek that ran into granddad's pond. The sheep wouldn't lay down or drink the water until he led them to the other side of the pond where the water was quiet and still.

Read verse 3: Animals or humans can create paths by walking the same route every day. I recall one evening granddad was leading the sheep into the barn and, even though they had done this hundreds of times, one of the sheep decided to wander and started following one of the cow paths that led in the opposite direction.

In this verse, the paths that lead to righteousness (right way of living) are also emphasized in Proverbs 4:19

Halftime Break:

Before reading the last 3 verses, notice an important change in David's psalm. In verses 1-3 he is talking *about* God by using the pronoun *he*. In verses 4-6 he is talking *to* God by using the pronoun *you*.

Read verse 4: The phrase "valley of the shadow of death" is usually emphasized when this scripture is read at funerals. Actually, some scholars say that may not be the most accurate translation. The Hebrew word for "shadows of death" means darkness or dark shadows. It does contain the same root word as the word death.

Sheep obviously don't understand the concept of death, but they are afraid of walking through dark valleys with shadows. Since many people fear death, it certainly may feel as if they are in a dark valley. God is always with us during these times to comfort us.

Keep in mind the importance of the word 'through'. Our dark valleys and troubles are temporary. We aren't going to stay there but are passing through them. They will end.

The word translated "evil" in Hebrew can mean harm or trouble of any kind. David is saying with God as our shepherd, we don't need to fear any kind of danger.

Since one of the most important jobs of a shepherd is to protect their sheep, they usually carried three tools: rod, staff, and sling. The *rod* was a sturdy wooden stick used to fight off wild animals and is a symbol of the Lord's strength and protection. The *staff* was a long, slender stick with a hook at the tip, and since sheep are known to be wanderers, it is a symbol of the Lord's guidance and lovingkindness.

The *sling* was composed of two strings of rope or leather attached to a leather pouch. We are most familiar with this weapon as it was used by David to kill Goliath.

There are 57 Hebrew words in Psalm 23. *There is one specific word that sits exactly in the middle of the psalm. 28 words lead up to it and 28 words follow it.*

This one vital Hebrew word in verse four, *im-mawd-ee*, translates to the phrase *"You are with me"*. This small part in the middle of the most beloved Psalm is the rock-solid promise that whether you are in a season of green pastures or in the darkest valley of your life, *God is with you!*

Read verse 5: 'Prepares a table' portrays his close relationship to God as an honored dinner guest. In the ancient East, a host was obligated to keep his visitors safe from enemies at all costs.

Flies are one of the worst enemies of sheep because they can't shake them off. The shepherd would use oil to soothe and heal them. 'Anoint my head with oil' can also refer to the ancient custom of hospitality of welcoming travelers by rubbing oil on their heads.

Read verse 6: The original term for 'goodness' means 'that which is pleasing or valuable'. And the word for 'mercy' means 'loyal or unfailing love'. A paraphrase of this last verse might be, 'Because You, Lord, are so good and love me so faithfully, I am sure I will live with

You forever.'

Final Thoughts on this Psalm of all Psalms

David had such a close relationship with God that he absolutely believed God would hear him when he prayed. And his prayer time also consisted of listening to God. Psalm 139:3-4 tells us that God hears and knows our voice.

I can't describe what the sound was like, but when granddad wanted the sheep to come to him, he would yell this strange sound that the sheep immediately recognized and knew what it meant.

Before Caller ID became available, when Lucy, Jon or Chris called me they might say something brief like, "Hi," and I knew exactly who it was. And if I simply responded with something like "How's it going?" they knew it was me. We talked so often we recognized each other's voice. *The more often we talk and listen to God, the closer our relationship will be with Him.*

In Psalm 23 we are reminded that as long as we have the Good Shepherd, we sheep don't need anyone or anything else. He is our protector and provider in every situation of our lives. And when we are hurting, He will heal our wounds and we can look forward to living with Him forever!

Positive Points to Ponder
- The story about Jesus leaving the ninety-nine sheep to find the one that is lost seems a little crazy, until YOU are the one who is trying to find your way back home.
- When others saw Sarah as just an old childless woman, God saw her as the mother of all nations.
When others saw David as just a young shepherd boy, God saw him as a great King. When God sees you, trust me . . . He REALLY sees you!

28

Find Peace in the Pit and Never Quit

It was called *The Greatest Show On Earth* by the Ringling Brothers Barnum and Bailey Circus. I was mesmerized from the time we walked in the lobby of the civic center until our family found our seats in the arena.

I loved every act and with something happening in all three rings simultaneously, it was captivating to keep up with all the action. The band played the entire time with clowns piling in and out of crazy cars, trapeze artists and high-wire walkers, dogs performing funny tricks, and performers standing on top of galloping horses.

But the moment I was waiting for finally arrived. The train of cars with bars let the lions out one-by-one and they entered the large, caged area as their trainer pointed to the place each was to sit. They were huge, enormous animals and the sound of their deafening roar created fear—even in our upper-level seats.

When I read the story of Daniel in the Lion's Den, this is an automatic flashback memory that brings the familiar story to life.

Snapshot Picture of Scripture (Daniel Chapter 6)

The prophet Daniel was the most outstanding administrator, so King Darius planned to promote him. His colleagues resented his success and favor from the king. Knowing he prayed to God three times a day, they convinced the king to make a decree that people who prayed to anyone other than the king would be thrown in a den of lions.

When Daniel heard about the declaration, he went to his usual place of prayer, and with the windows open, continued his usual practice of praying to God.

The men caught Daniel praying and told the King, who now had no choice but to have him arrested and thrown in the den of lions. The king did not want anything to happen to Daniel and told him he hoped his God would keep him safe.

The king was so worried about Daniel he couldn't eat and stayed awake all night. At the break of dawn, he ran to the lion's den and found the angels had shut the mouths of the lions and Daniel was safe—not even a scratch.

Easier to say than do.

Pit #1. As I read this amazing story of faith and perseverance, it is easy to think I would react the same way. But in reality, there is a good possibility my prayer would go something like: "God, why are you letting this happen to me?" or "Please get me out of here!" or "God, I've been so loyal to you. This is just not fair."

Do you know what he prayed for? Daniel 6:10b tells us he spoke prayers of gratitude! Are you kidding me? He is 80 years old, been thrown in a pit of lions, and he thanked God. He wasn't denying his circumstances. He was turning to God in the midst of them. *We can't always fix our circumstances, but we can always fix our eyes on God!*

Pit #2. In Genesis chapter 39, we find the life-changing story of Joseph being thrown in a pit and later sold into slavery by his jealous brothers. But even as a slave he developed valuable skills and was put in charge of his master's household.

Later he was falsely accused and thrown in prison. Eventually he was put in charge of the whole prison. He refused to quit and persevered in the pit and in prison. Years later he forgave and reconciled with his brothers and gave them and their families land on which to live. All because *he refused to quit in the pit.*

Just Don't Quit
Success is failure turned inside out,
The silver tint to the clouds of doubt;
It's hard to tell how close you are,
It may be near when it seems so far;
So stick to the fight when you're hardest hit,
With God's guidance and grace—*never quit!*

Pit #3. In his book, *In A Pit With A Lion On A Snowy Day* by pastor and author Mark Batterson, he shares a 'pit story' found in 2 Samuel 23:20-21 that has a totally different, but important, perspective.

It is the true story of an ancient warrior named Benaiah who chased a lion into a pit, and he came out the victor! For most people that situation wouldn't just be a problem. It would possibly be the last problem they ever faced. Like David ran toward Goliath to confront him, Benaiah ran toward the lion and chased him into a pit.

He encourages us to face our times of fear and persevere by being bold and maintaining our focus and faith. Poor odds pale in comparison with an omnipotent God.

Your greatest regret at the end of your life will be the lions you didn't chase. You don't want to look back at the risks not taken, opportunities not seized, and the dreams not pursued. *Unleash the lion-chaser within you!*

Perseverance is getting up more times than you're knocked down.

Learning how to be strong and persevere can come from an unexpected source—like the birth of a baby giraffe. In his book, *A View from the Zoo,* Gary Richmond describes how a newborn giraffe learns its first lesson of not quitting or giving up.

Bringing a giraffe into the world is a tall order—literally. A baby giraffe falls 10 feet from its mother's womb and usually lands on its back. Within seconds it rolls over and tucks its legs under its lanky body. Then the mother introduces its offspring to the reality of life.

The mother giraffe lowers her head long enough to take a quick look. Then she positions herself directly over her calf and then does the most unreasonable thing. She swings her long, pendulous leg outward and kicks her baby so that it is sent sprawling head over heels.

After many unsuccessful attempts the calf finally gets up and stands on its wobbly legs. Then the mother does something that seems almost cruel and difficult to understand. She kicks it off its feet again. Why? *She wants it to remember how it got up!* In the wild, giraffes must be able to get up quickly to stay with the herd.

Use your pit as a platform!

Getting knocked down or finding yourself in a pit is part of life. Most likely you haven't spent time in a physical pit but during tough times have thought, "My life is the pits."

If you don't experience seasons of pits in life, you won't have a testimony to share about the power of God and how He helped you climb out. *So, use your pit as a platform.*

Peter and the other apostles were chained in prison, beaten several times a day, went days without food, and when released continued to preach the message of Jesus in the temple courts after being strictly ordered by the high priest not to teach in His name. When brought before the Sanhedrin to be questioned by the high priest for their actions, Peter and the apostles replied, "We must obey God rather than human beings…" (Acts 5:29). *They persevered and had 'peace in the pit and never quit'!*

Positive Points to Ponder
- No matter how bad things may seem, don't quit on God because He never quits on you.
- Perseverance through tough times can be a slow process. But the end results are worth it. How else could a couple of snails make it to the ark?

29

Different Names Mean the Same

I never understood why the teachers' class list of students stated their last name first then the first name. My fourth-grade teacher, Mrs. Kelly, apparently thought it was unique and a little humorous that my name, Charles J. King, was listed as King, Charles.

Most teachers ask what name students would like to be called during the school year. But for some reason, she got a charge out of using this format for me. I can still hear her asking, "King Charles, what do you have as the answer to number seven?" Naturally my friends caught on and I was quickly known in elementary school as 'The King'.

Later in high school, I was nicknamed 'Pretzel'. As one of several football players was getting up after a tackle, the coach jokingly shared with the team that my body gets twisted in so many different positions, I look like a pretzel.

Our names and nicknames are important, but in biblical times the meaning of someone's name was vital to their identity. Barnabus means 'son of encouragement' and Abraham means 'father of nations'.

Precise differences in a name or title may be open for interpretation. Jesus' name in Hebrew, "Yeshua", is a transliteration to English as Joshua and means "to deliver, to rescue, or the Lord saves".

Just as meaningful as someone's name is understanding who they are. Jesus first asked the disciples who the people or crowds say He is. Then He asked them, "Who do you say that I am?" (Luke 9:20 ESV). The gospel of John includes seven descriptions shared by Jesus Himself identifying who He is.

Snapshot Picture of Scripture
    The 7 'I am' Statements of Jesus
1. "I am the bread of life." (John 6:35)
2. "I am the light of the world." (John 8:12)
3. "I am the door." (John 10:7)

4. "I am the good shepherd." (John 10:11)
5. "I am the resurrection and the life." (John 11:25)
6. "I am the way, the truth, and the life." (John 14:6)
7. "I am the true vine." (John 15:1)

Each of these statements by Jesus not only enhances our understanding of who He is, but also links Him with the Old Testament revelation of God. In the Old Testament God reveals Himself to Moses: "I AM WHO I AM." In Judaism, "I AM" is unquestionably understood as a name for God. Jesus was identifying Himself as God.

It is important that beginning with the first 'I am', He begins a pattern that continued through the gospel of John. He makes a statement about who He is and backs it up by something He *does*. For example:

He feeds the 5,000 to show He is the Bread of Life.

He gives a blind man his sight to show He is the Light of the World.

He changes water into wine to show He is the True Vine.

He raises Lazarus from the dead to show He is the Resurrection and the Life.

Notice that His name is "I am." Not "I was," or "I might be," or "I may get to it." He is in control. He always has been and always will be!

Bring out the bread (and butter and jelly).

Jesus began His list of ways to describe Himself by declaring He is the Bread of Life.

Similar to many families, at our home bread was considered a necessary menu item for most meals. I'm nowhere close to a bread chef but can visualize toast, biscuits, rolls, cornbread, breadsticks, buns (for burgers, hotdogs, and subs), sourdough, rye, and 100's of varieties of sliced loaf bread.

Bread is considered such a basic food necessity that we sometimes hear or use the phrase "breaking bread together" to indicate sharing a meal with someone. Before Lucy or I go to the grocery store, there are two items we always make sure we have–milk and bread.

Bread is not exactly a new food item. When the Jews were wandering in the desert for 40 years, God miraculously rained down "bread from heaven" (manna) to sustain them.

Inhabitants in the Middle East during the life of Jesus ate a lot of bread. Usually, it was made with wheat or barley flour and sometimes seasoned with oil or herbs. Besides the simple round loaf and flatbread, there were cakes with grapes or honey. (Think grape jelly or apple butter.) And with the wine and food at the Last Supper, Jesus and the disciples ate unleavened bread.

Not what they were expecting.

The day before Jesus said He was the 'bread of life', He fed 5,000 men, plus women and children, with just some bread and a couple of fish. Out of this huge crowd only about 400 followed Him to hear more about the Good News. In fact, He accused the crowd of only following Him to get a 'free meal'.

Of the 11 closest disciples, only three followed Him deeper in the garden as He prayed. And only one of the 11 who were left stood with Him at the cross. Jesus was clearly not what they were expecting.

Most of the Pharisees, and many of his followers, had a difficult time believing who He claimed to be. In C. S. Lewis' book, *Liar, Lord, or Lunatic,* he points out that 'this means one of three things; He or the disciples are lying, He is insane, or He is truly God in flesh'.

If Jesus were physically on earth today, there is a good possibility we would see a headline on social media and news outlets that reads something like:

Local Carpenter with Extremist Views Continues to Spread Disinformation Deemed Harmful By Religious Experts

When we remind ourselves of the background of Jesus, it is not difficult to understand why so many did not follow and believe in Him—in spite of the miracles John said were signs that He was the Messiah.

Jesus was born in an obscure village, the child of a peasant teenage girl. He worked until He was 30 in a carpenter's shop. Then for three years He was a traveling teacher and preacher. He never traveled more than 200 miles from His hometown. He never wrote a book and never held an office.

His friends abandoned Him. He was rejected by His own family and people in His hometown. One of His closest followers denied that he knew Him, and another betrayed Him, resulting in His physical death.

He was nailed on a cross, and when He died, He was homeless and so poor He was buried in a borrowed tomb.

While physically on earth, some accepted and many rejected Jesus, but history proves there is something sacred and special about the name of Jesus. Bill and Gloria Gaither describe in their song *There's Something About That Name:*

> Jesus, Jesus, Jesus; There's just something about that name.
> Master, Savior, Jesus; like the fragrance after the rain.
> Jesus, Jesus, Jesus; Let all Heaven and earth proclaim,
> > Kings and kingdoms will all pass away;
> > But there's something about that name.

When Jesus was crucified, a plaque with a title was placed over His head on the cross. It was written in three languages and in English translates to, "Jesus the Nazarene, King of the Jews." Part of the popular message describing Jesus as our King by Rev. S. M. Lockwood is titled...

That's My King

"No means of measure can define His limitless love. He's the centerpiece of civilization. He strengthens and sustains. He's the wellspring of wisdom. He's the doorway of deliverance.

He's the path of peace. He's the roadway of righteousness. He's the highway of holiness. He's the gateway of glory. He's the master of the mighty.

He's the captain of the conquerors. He's the head of the heroes. He's the overseer of the overcomers. He's incomprehensible. He's invincible. And He's irresistible. Yes–*That's* My King!"

Bread for us today!

We are reminded that the "bread of life" means spiritual bread and not dinner rolls, biscuits, cornbread, or bagels. He still offers this life-giving bread to us.

And if we eat, He promises "we will never go hungry." It's like an **'All You Can Eat Bread of Life Buffet'**! And then He adds that we will never go thirsty. In other words, we will go from **'Running Out to Running Over'**!

2,000 years later, billions gather in His name. No one has affected and transformed the lives of so many people around the world as Jesus–the 'bread of life'!

Positive Points to Ponder
- Love doesn't just sit still like a rock, but like bread, it has to be made and worked on every day to remain fresh and sustain life.
- Enjoying fresh baked bread makes a good meal. But when you share it with someone it becomes a feast.

30

A Lawyer Looking for a Loophole

Based on the following description, can you name the television program? Each episode begins with a man walking onto the set while singing to piano accompaniment wearing a sport coat and tie. He walks to a closet and hangs up his sport coat, replacing it with a sweater that zips up the front–still singing.

He then sits down, takes off his loafers, and replaces them with sneakers. One final give-away hint. A few of the lyrics to the show's theme song he is singing include:

> It's a beautiful day in the neighborhood,
> A beautiful day for a neighbor,
> Would you be mine?
> Could you be mine?
> Please won't you be my neighbor?

If you recognize the lyrics, there is a good chance you're humming the tune to yourself right now. It's the theme song to *Mister Rogers' Neighborhood*, one of the most popular children's programs in history. It was televised on PBS, ran for 33 years, and Fred Rogers, the host, was also a Christian minister.

We may think the sweater and sneakers were a little out of style, but his message to children and adults is more relevant today than ever. It comes directly from the ever-familiar parable of the Good Samaritan and relates to one of Jesus' most vital messages about the importance of loving others.

Snapshot Picture of Scripture (Luke 10:25-37)

After a lawyer asked Jesus how he could inherit eternal life, He responded by asking the man what the Mosaic Law states. The lawyer answered by quoting Deuteronomy 6:5, which says to love the LORD your God with all your heart, soul, strength, and mind. The law expert then quotes Leviticus 19:18, that you must also love your neighbor.

But when Jesus tells him he was right, the man wants to justify his actions, so he asks Jesus to define who his neighbor is. Jesus explained by sharing a parable. Interesting that Luke is the only gospel in which this popular parable is recorded.

The story begins with a Jewish man traveling from Jerusalem to Jericho where he is attacked, robbed, stripped of his clothes, and left for dead. A priest sees him but walks past him and does nothing to help him. Then a Levite sees him and does the same thing.

But when a Samaritan (Samaritans were despised by the Jews) sees him, he feels compassion for him. He soothes his wounds with olive oil and wine and bandages them. He puts him on his own donkey, takes him to an inn, and then pays the innkeeper so he could stay as long as needed.

Then Jesus asks the lawyer which of the three men is his neighbor. The lawyer despises Samaritans so much, he can't even bring himself to say the word and instead says 'the one who showed mercy'. But Jesus wanted to make sure the man got this point and told him to go and do the same thing to others.

Focus on the facts—not on finding fault.

The lawyer in the parable was an expert in religious law. When Jesus asked him what the law stated regarding neighbors, he knew the Torah well and quoted it word-for-word. He also knew that *neighbor* was defined as a fellow Jew and the Hebrews' definition was someone who lives near someone. The law specifically excluded Samaritans as they were considered half-breed, low-life, unclean outcasts of society.

The route from Jerusalem to Jericho is a winding, dangerous path that descends about 3,000 feet where attacks by robbers were common. The man's clothes were his most valuable possessions, so he literally lost all he had.

Scholars debate different reasons why the priest and the Levite didn't stop to help. Perhaps they were too busy or simply didn't care. For whatever reason, they didn't follow Jesus' teachings of loving their neighbor and the 'least of these'.

The pompous people and their new compassionate pastor:

A congregation that 'was dressed to impress in their Sunday go-to-meeting best' hurriedly walked past the homeless man sitting on the front steps of their church. They entered with excitement and mingled with each other before the service started wondering what their new pastor would be like.

The homeless man decided to go inside and asked several people if they would give him some money for food, but no one offered and most just looked down and walked away. He decided to sit down in a pew, and the ushers quickly asked him to please have a seat in the back of the sanctuary.

The big moment arrived, and the announcement was made to please welcome their new pastor. The congregation erupted into applause. But when the 'homeless' man in the back started walking down the aisle and eventually stepped on the platform, the applause stopped as reality hit them where it hurts most—in their hearts.

As the new pastor removed his fake beard and disheveled clothes, there was total silence. Mouths fell open, and many eyes filled with tears. The pastor smiled, shared the parable of the Good Samaritan and how love and mercy is more than just attending church. It requires taking action by *loving our neighbor.*

Confession is good for *my* soul.

Jesus explained in Matthew 25:31-40 that when his followers care for the *least of these*—those who are hungry, thirsty, oppressed, need clothes, in prison, or are sick—*we are doing it for Him.*

One of the most meaningful personal experiences of helping 'the least of these' occurred when my long-time friend, Tom, and I took a group of high school and college youth on a mission trip to feed and minister to the homeless in Washington DC.

What a blessing it was to see this group of young people, including our sons Jon, Chris, and Tee, find and feed people sleeping under plastic tarps, in garbage bags, and under bridges and porches.

It made a powerful impact on all of us. Tom shared a profound thought with me as we were returning home. He said, "I've probably been to DC over 100 times, but I'll never see this city again with the same eyes. God has truly opened the eyes of my heart for the homeless."

But did you notice something about my experience? The verbs are past tense. In other words, I did most of those things in the past. I trust you will learn, or be reminded with my confession, that Jesus did not ask us to put love into action only during specific times of the year or a season of our life. We are to look for daily opportunities to help and serve our 'neighbors'.

Sample signs from the Samaritan.
1. *Love knows no boundaries or limits.* Your neighbor is most likely someone who doesn't look like you, doesn't dress like you, and doesn't vote like you. The question may not be '*who* is my neighbor' but instead, '*how* can I be a neighbor to others?'.
2. *We can also learn from the lawyer.* He knew the Torah well. We need to continually learn the lessons Christ taught. And he demonstrated his respect for Jesus by standing up and calling Him rabbi (teacher).
3. *Our love for God is reflected by how we love our neighbors.* In fact, we can't love God without loving our neighbors.

Positive Points to Ponder
- A good neighbor indeed is helping anyone in need.
- The happiest people I know are people who don't even think about being happy. They just think about being a good neighbor to everyone, and the happiness sort of sneaks in the back door while they are busy loving people.

31

He Can Inspire and Ignite Your Faith-Fire

In 1859 French acrobat Charles Blondin strung a rope across Niagara Falls and announced that he would walk a tightrope from one side to the other—over 1,000 feet of rope about 200 feet above the raging river below. A huge crowd showed up and working everyone into a frenzy asked if they had faith and believed he could do it.

They screamed in response, "Yes, we have faith and believe!" After hours of patiently inching his way across the two-inch cable, he finally stepped safely off on the opposite side to the screams and applause of everyone.

He finally quieted the crowd and asked if they had faith and believed he could carry someone in a wheelbarrow to the other side. Again, the crowd responded, "Yes, we have faith and believe."

Then he requested, "I need someone to step forward and volunteer to ride in the wheelbarrow." The crowd became deathly silent, and all eyes looked down. No one stepped forward.

There is a distinct difference in *saying* we have faith and putting our beliefs into action by *taking the first step*.

The next three chapters address the important topics of faith, hope, and love separately, while understanding they are intertwined and connected.

Faith, Hope, and Love

When we throw babies up in the air they giggle and laugh because they know and believe we will catch them. That is *faith*.

Every night we go to bed with no assurance we will get up the next morning and yet we set the alarm. That is *hope*.

We see our world suffering and yet we get married and have children. That is *love*.

Snapshot Picture of Scripture. (Luke 5:17-26)

One day Jesus was teaching and healing people in a packed-out home where He was staying. Several Pharisees and teachers of the law came from surrounding villages and were standing in the crowd.

Then several men showed up carrying their paralyzed friend on a mat hoping to lay him before Jesus so he could be healed. But the crowd was so large they couldn't get inside the house, so they climbed up on the roof, tore a hole in it, and lowered their friend on his mat into the middle of the crowd—right in front of Jesus.

Jesus saw their great faith and decided to start the healing process by forgiving him of his sins. He then turned to the man and told him to get up, take his mat and go home.

Imagine the shock of the people as they are watching Jesus teach and heal when straw and tiles start falling from the ceiling. They look up and see daylight shining through the hole that is being dug out of the roof. Eventually they see the faces of the men looking down at them as they lower their friend.

Visualize their shock as they watch the man stand up, grab his mat, and start walking through the crowd–praising God, laughing with joy, and giving high fives and hugs to everyone as he leaves.

With a little help from my friends.

Let's temporarily make this story our story and picture ourselves as the man on the mat with his faith-filled friends.

I'm thinking of several special individuals and also a few groups of amazing friends with whom I'm blessed—church, FCA Board, and our weekly men's Bible Study group.

And I am reminded of my life-long friend Bill Smith calling me years ago to share that a group of our high school buddies were getting together for the weekend. In spite of numerous life changes involving families, distances, and career changes, we have continued this tradition annually for over 35 years!

I absolutely believe if I were the 'man on the mat', all the friends mentioned above would do whatever it takes to get me to the doctor—including cutting a hole in the roof so I could be healed. (Although I admit some of them would have a little fun and laugh as they let me down yelling "oops", pretending they had dropped me.)

Back to the Basics. What exactly *is* faith?

Before we look at some formal or Biblical definitions, one of my real-world favorite ways to define faith is simply:

> Faith is acting like something IS so,
> even though it's NOT YET so,
> in order that it might BE so,
> simply because God SAYS so!

It is not faith if you already have it figured out. It usually will not make sense and may seem illogical. *Faith starts where our understanding ends.* Faith is not mere intellectual assent, and it is not temporal. Temporal faith is trusting God for temporary emergencies or needs in life such as asking for help in times of sickness, financial pressures, or relationship issues.

Then after we get through these experiences, our prayers substantially decrease. Feel free to say 'ouch' with me as I just stepped on my own toes with those statements.

When I began seeking truth on my personal spiritual journey, I would ask questions, and if the believer didn't know the answer, their typical response was something like, "I don't know, but you just gotta have faith, Jerry. You just gotta have faith."

That didn't really work for me because that is a *blind faith* which requires no thinking, reasoning, or using the God-given intellectual capacities of our mind. We are born with a natural quest to find spiritual truth.

In their book, *The Handbook of Christian Apologetics*, authors Peter Kreeft and Ronald Tacelli offer the following relationship between faith and reason: "Faith and reason are allies. We do not believe reason should usurp the primacy of faith, hope and love. When faith comes first, understanding follows. Reason is the friend of faith."

A solid and simple definition of faith is found in Scripture and recognized as the 'Hall of Fame Heroes of Faith'. "Faith is the confidence that what we hope for will actually happen; it gives us assurance about things we cannot see" (Hebrews 11:1 NLT).

Martin Luther, leader of the Protestant Reformation, shares, "Faith is a living, daring, confidence in God's grace, so sure and certain that a man could stake his life on it a thousand times."

Facets and Factors of Faith:
- **Trust** is perhaps one of the most essential characteristics of faith in the Bible. One of the Hebrew words for faith, *aman*, means "trust, believe, be faithful." Look at a coin or dollar bill and search for the phrase we carry with us every day as a reminder: "In God We Trust".

    God knows exactly *what* you need, how *much* you need, and *when* you need it. Whatever you are going through, He didn't bring you this far to leave you. He will not fail you. *Trust Him!*
- **Belief** in the fact that God through Christ is the way to eternal life and begins in our hearts. In Romans 10, Paul says to 'declare with your mouth and to believe in your heart'. Oxford professor C. S. Lewis states, "I believe in Christianity as I believe that the sun rises—not only because I see it, but because by it I see everything else."
- **Waiting** is one of God's most effective ways to teach us and test our faith. Ever watched an advertisement and the announcer says, "But wait, there's more!" Sometimes your faith can make you look foolish–until it starts raining. Just ask Noah. Neighbors and friends laughed when he shared that God told him a huge flood was coming and to build a big boat that could float. It wasn't even drizzling when he and his family started building the ark that took 70-75 years of waiting and working.

Many times if we don't see something happening, we don't think God is doing anything. Waiting is when faith develops. *The presence of silence never equals the absence of God.*

True Story: As the result of not receiving rain for over three years, a town was experiencing a severe drought. Crops were drying up, and clean drinking water was scarce. The leaders decided they had to do something, and it would be a good idea for everyone to meet together and have a day of prayer.

The big day arrived and most everyone showed up for prayer. *But only one little boy arrived carrying an umbrella. That* is *true faith*. Expecting, trusting, and believing that God will do something miraculous.

Real faith is a faith of action. *Doing a deed and not just reciting a creed.* Jesus' brother James stated, "Show me your faith without deeds, and I will show you my faith by my deeds" (James 2:18 NIV).

When your path is not clear, take a step without fear.

At the age of 15, Jennifer Rothschild was diagnosed with a rare, degenerative eye disease. The door to her dreams of becoming a commercial artist slowly started to close and she eventually became totally blind.

But because of her strong trust in God, she had no choice but to take a step of faith in another direction. When she reads the verse in 2 Corinthians 5:7 (NASB), "We walk by faith, not by sight" the words are a reflection of how she lives.

Since taking that first step, she has written numerous books for Bible Studies including, *Lessons Learned in the Dark: Walking By Faith*. She shares, "Walking by faith is living in a reality not yet seen. Relying on sight—as paradoxical as it sounds—blinds us to God's best. Most of us never learn to walk by faith until we learn to walk in the dark."

Has a door closed for you? If so, it's time to take that first step and walk by faith. Sometimes God allows doors to close because it's time to move forward. He knows you won't take a step until circumstances force you to move. *It's time to stop talking and start walking!*

Positive Points to Ponder
- Faith is taking the first step when you can't see the whole staircase.
- Faith sees the invisible, believes the unbelievable, and receives the impossible.

32

Heavenly Hope Can Help You Cope

Reading the giant headline at the top of a full-page newspaper ad, it seemed too good to be true.

We Pay Cash for Old Coins and Jewelry!

My 50-year-old coin collection from elementary school was stored in a box in our basement, just waiting to be cashed in for big-time money. This is why I saved it all these years.

I ran down the steps, found my collection, and the more time I spent looking through it, the longer my wish-list and the bigger my dreams grew.

I owned Buffalo nickels as old as 1918, Mercury Head Dimes as far back as 1926, and copper Lincoln Wheat Pennies from 1909–including three rare 1943 steel pennies.

I excitedly shared the situation with Lucy and explained that with all the money my collection was probably worth, I may need a Wells Fargo truck to escort me back home.

As I drove to the hotel where the appraisers were located, I couldn't help but dream about what I hoped we could do with the money. After we pay off our mortgage and travel to Europe, Italy, and the Holy Land, we will purchase a second home at the lake and possibly another one at the beach.

The cordial lady at the table started flipping through my coin books with fingers flowing in a blur on her calculator. After a few minutes she politely shared that the face value of the coins was $73.27.

I thought something must be wrong, and when I asked how much cash she would pay me, considering the coins' age and condition, she again shared the same answer, $73.27. She then looked past me to the people in line and asked the same one-word question my barber uses, "Next?"

After I gathered my coin books, started my slow walk to the car, and had a disappointing drive home, it became clear—I had based my wishes and dreams on *false hope*. I know better and am familiar with scripture telling us to 'lay-up treasures in heaven' but was still guilty of getting caught up in the moment and putting temporary hope ahead of eternal truth.

Thankfully, followers of Christ can base our hopes and dreams on Him. And the beginning of the most meaningful story of hope in the history of mankind begins with His amazing birth—the Baby that changed everything!

Snapshot Picture of Scripture (Luke 1:26-35; 2:1-20)

Mary is a virgin and engaged to marry Joseph. An angel appears to Mary and tells her the Lord has chosen her to conceive a Son and He is to be called Jesus.

At first Mary is afraid and confused, wondering how this is possible since she is a virgin. The angel then assures her not to be afraid, and she will supernaturally conceive by the Holy Spirit.

During this time the government was taking a census, and the heads of all households were required to return to their ancestral community to register.

Joseph and his pregnant wife Mary had no choice but to make the 90-mile journey on foot through rugged mountains to Bethlehem. Not exactly an enjoyable vacation trip.

Completely exhausted after five days of traveling, they finally arrived. But the city was crowded with so many people they could not find a place to spend the night.

They are finally offered a stable where the animals stay. Despite popular Christmas card pictures, stables were usually dark, dingy, dirty caves. It was in these humble surroundings that Mary gave birth to Jesus, the Messiah. She then wraps Him in strips of cloth and places Him in the only crib available—a manger feeding trough for animals.

The best birth announcement ever! An angel appears to nearby shepherds as they watch over their sheep that night and announces the breaking news that a Savior is born. At first they were terrified but soon hurriedly ran off to find the Baby. They shared their experience with Joseph and Mary, and the exciting news that the Messiah is born quickly spreads like wildfire.

Noteworthy Notes About the Nativity:

The story of Jesus' birth is known as the Nativity. The birth of hundreds of characters in the Old Testament are recorded and all point to the birth of Christ. *After Christ is born, not a single birth is recorded in the entire rest of the Bible!*

Engaged. The word used often is *betrothed,* or pledged, and in biblical times the couple was considered married but had not yet held the wedding ceremony. Like most brides-to-be, Mary was 14-15 years old, and her marriage to Joseph was probably arranged by the parents. So, when she became pregnant before they married, Joseph didn't want to embarrass her and considered calling it off.

Shepherds. Many well-known biblical figures were at one time shepherds–Abraham, Jacob, Moses, and David. Shepherds were considered one of the lowliest jobs and were looked down on by most. They took care of animals and were known to be dirty and smell like the creatures they protected. Jesus called himself the Good Shepherd, and shepherds were the first group of people God chose to announce the birth of Jesus.

Sheep and Lambs: We sometimes overlook the importance of why shepherds watched their sheep at night near Bethlehem. One reason is that it was 'lambing season'. Unlike humans, lambs are only born during one season, and this is the only time shepherds stay up all night watching their sheep give birth to their lambs.

It wasn't a coincidence they were near Jerusalem–the place for the sacrifice of unblemished lambs in the temple. Once the sheep's blood was completely spilled for all the sins, the temple priests would return to the people and proclaim, *"It is finished."* I find this parallelism to Christ to be absolutely amazing.

The "Lamb of God" was also born in Bethlehem, was without blemishes (sin), and was led to Jerusalem to be sacrificed. *When He was crucified, His last recorded words are the identical words the temple priests proclaimed, "It is finished!"*

The Anchor: Christian Symbol of Hope.

The anchor has been a symbol of hope among Christians since the days of the early church. A ship's anchor allows the vessel to remain fixed and unmoving regardless of the conditions of the sea.

Our hope and faith in Christ keep us from becoming "like a wave of the sea, blown and tossed by the wind" (James 1:6).

The author of Hebrews shares, "We have this hope as an anchor for the soul, firm and secure" (Hebrews 6:19 NIV). It is a powerful hope on which we can always depend. This same passage reminds us that 'we can have great confidence as we hold on to the hope that lies before us'.

Hope for the soul.
In 1873, two years after the Great Chicago Fire, the family of Horatio Spafford boarded a steamship for a family vacation in England. Because of business responsibilities, he was unable to travel with them.

While crossing the Atlantic, the ship was struck by an iron sailing vessel, killing 226 people, including all four of his daughters. His wife, Anna, survived the tragedy.

Shortly afterwards as Spafford was traveling to meet his grieving wife, he was called to the deck and told they were crossing the area where his daughters perished in the sea.

Understandably distraught, he openly wept. But as a believer he knew his hope was based on the anchor of Christ and that his soul and life would be well. At this time, he wrote one of the most beloved and comforting of all hymns.

It Is Well With My Soul
When peace like a river attendeth my way,
When sorrows like sea billows roll;
Whatever my lot, Thou hast taught me to say,
It is well, it is well with my soul.

More than one kind of hope.
- *False Temporal Hope*: Optimism not supported by reality or facts, temporary and may be misguided. "I hope…I won the lottery; she will go out with me. (Or "I hope my old coin collection is worth thousands.")
- *General Hope:* Generally optimistic most of the time. Viewing life positively and a belief that most situations will work out or turn out well.
- *Living Hope*: A virtuous quality of a believer because it contains no doubt, always trusting in God's faithfulness and presence no matter the circumstances. We don't just *wish* we will go to heaven. The Bible says in I John 5:13 we can *know it* with certainty. Our hope is not simply an *act* of confident

expectation but also the *object* of it.

When you feel discouraged or in a state of hopelessness, remember that genuine hope in Christ will strengthen you for the challenges you face in life because we see those challenges through the lens of God's character—faith, hope, and love.

"Those who hope in the Lord will renew their strength" (Isaiah 40:31a). *Hope began with Christ's birth and lives forever because of His resurrection!*

Positive Points to Ponder
- Believe like Mary.
  Trust like Joseph.
  Hope like the shepherds.
  Seek like the wise men.
  Worship like the angels.
  Love like Jesus!
- Some people only see a hopeless end. But a believer sees an endless hope. When you feel like you are drowning in a sea of hopelessness, don't give up. Remember, our Lifeguard can walk on water!

33

Note of Love from Above

As a fourth grader I watched out of the corner of my eye as she secretly passed a note to the student sitting next to her, who continued the procedure until it traveled across the classroom and finally reached me.

Holding the note under my desk out of sight from our teacher, I slowly opened it and read these words:

I love you. Do you love me? Check which one and return.

___ Yes

___ No

I decided this question was way too deep for a boy in the fourth grade. The highlight of my day was trading baseball cards, and a few were clamped to my bicycle tire with a clothespin to make it sound like a motor while pedaling.

So, I decided to have a little fun by adding a third option. I wrote the word 'Maybe', put a check beside it, and sent it back across the classroom. After reading my additional choice, the puzzled look on her face was worth a thousand words.

Of course, every student who played a part in returning the note read it and thought it was pretty funny, and I was considered almost cool. She never spoke to me again the rest of the school year, so I guess our case of puppy love was not quite as deep as she thought.

Since the entire 66 books of the Bible focus on *God's love,* let's look at a few scripture passages that reveal some valuable insights regarding the unlimited love of God and His Son, Jesus the Christ.

Snapshot Picture of Scripture

"For God so loved the world that He gave his only begotten son, that whoever believes in Him should not perish but have everlasting life" (John 3:16 NKJV).

"This is how we know what love is: Jesus Christ laid down His life for us. And we ought to lay down our lives for our brothers and sisters" (1 John 3:16 NIV).

"Love is patient and kind; love does not envy or boast; it is not arrogant or rude. It does not insist on its own way; it is not irritable or resentful; it does not rejoice at wrongdoing but rejoices with the truth. Love bears all things, believes all things, hopes all things, endures all things" (1 Corinthians 13:4-7 ESV).

"Three things will last forever–faith, hope, and love–and the greatest of these is love" (1 Corinthians 13:13 NLT).

It is worth noting that the first two passages above are in separate books and written by the apostle John. Both are found in the same chapter and verse (3:16), and both verses share the same message–God sacrificed his Son for us.

The last two passages are written by Paul to the people in the church in Corinth who are having some disagreements with each other. He reminds them (and us) about the importance of loving each other and what love really means.

1 Corinthians 13 is known as the 'love chapter' and is commonly read at weddings. Verse 13 gives us Paul's insight that *believers must have all three–faith, hope, and love–but love is the foundation.*

You've lost that loving feeling.

In today's culture and society, the word *love* is used to describe so many situations, relationships, and feelings. We don't need to search long for past popular songs through the years that view love differently, as described in their titles.

A few oldie-goldie reminders: *All You Need Is Love, Love Me Tender Love Me True, I Just Called to Say I Love You, I Want to Know What Love Is,* and *Crazy Little Thing Called Love.*

And there are many spirit-filled songs with titles such as: *Love Lifted Me, Jesus Loves Me, I Love You Lord,* and *I Love to Tell the Story.*

We frequently use the word in casual expressions: love a parade, love food, love sports or music, love is blind, no love lost, love handles, love of my life, and the ad slogan of a mouthwash–the taste you love to hate.

What the Word says about *love*:

The Bible tells us that 'love is of God' and 'God is love'. In other words, love is a fundamental characteristic of who God is. Everything

God does is influenced by His love.

We find four different types of love in the Bible.

- **Philia—Brotherly Love:** Love found in close relationships, such as friends. The city of Philadelphia was so named as the 'city of brotherly love'.
- **Storge—Family Love:** Love between family members.
- **Eros—Romantic Love:** Love that is romantically emotional.
- **Agape—Divine Love:** An unconditional, unlimited, sacrificial love that is found between God and Jesus, believers and God, and among believers.

In the Apostle Paul's first letter to the people in the church at Corinth, he describes seven things that love is and does, (passage above.) Love is a noun and a verb so he not only defines what it *is,* but what we should and should not *do.*

God demonstrated what sacrifice really means in John 3:16 when He gave his "only begotten Son" for us. The phrase "only begotten" translates the Greek word *monogenes* as 'only' or 'one and only'. Surveys show that this verse of scripture is the most widely recognized in the entire Bible.

Perhaps you remember a man with a wild multi-colored wig holding a bold sign at sporting events years ago that simply read, "John 3:16". It was his personal way of sharing the Good News.

The following story is one that leads us to realize how a loving God must have felt when He sacrificed His Son.

The Ultimate Sacrifice of A Loving Father.

In 1937 John Griffith worked as a bridge operator for a railroad. His eight-year-old son, Greg, loved to spend time with his dad at work fishing and watching the people on the trains passing by.

One day John realized his son wasn't fishing. As he looked around, to his horror he saw his son climbing around on the gears of the train tracks.

He hurried outside to rescue his son but just then heard a fast-approaching passenger train filled with over 400 people. He yelled to Greg, but the noise of the oncoming train made it impossible for the boy to hear him.

All of a sudden, John Griffith realized his horrible dilemma. If he changed the gears on the tracks to rescue his son, the train would crash–killing all aboard. If he saved the train, his son would be crushed in the gears. He made the horrific decision to pull the gear and save the people on the train.

It is said as the train went by, he could see the faces of the passengers–some reading, some even waving. All of them unaware or uncaring of the sacrifice he had just made for them.

This story portrays the amazing sacrificial love God the Father made for us when He sent His Son to die for all humanity. *When Christ tells us to love Him and love others it is not only the greatest commandment, but the most rewarding way to live!*

Positive Points to Ponder
- God loves you more in a moment than anyone else could in a lifetime.
- God is not yet done writing the best love story for YOU!

34

One Main Rule in the Rabbi's School

As a career educator I will assure you that the 1960's high school conduct rules were quite different than today. A few prime examples: 1. No talking in class unless called upon by the teacher. 2. Stand quietly in a straight line in the cafeteria. 3. No holding hands or showing physical affection of any kind. 4. No chewing gum in class.

Sitting in ninth grade English class one day, my teacher's words startled me. Actually, they woke me up. "Mr. King, please tell me you are not chewing gum in my class again. You know the rule–three strikes and you're out. You need to go to the principal's office and tell him you broke the 'no chewing gum in class' rule three times."

After swallowing three sticks of Juicy Fruit gum as I walked down the hall, I shared my crime with our principal. He reached into his desk drawer, handed me a shoebox and putty knife, and calmly said, "Follow me." (To my best recollection, his words were not stated with the same tone of voice Jesus used when He called his disciples.)

He then led me to the auditorium where about 50 classmates were in study hall. He instructed me to use the putty knife to scrape chewing gum off the bottom of all 800 seats and to bring the box of recycled gum to him when finished.

Needless to say, with my classmates loudly inviting me to come scrape Dentyne, Peppermint, and Bazooka Joe gum off their seats, it was a humbling and humiliating experience that never needed to be repeated.

One of the most familiar passages of scripture, which includes Jesus' guidelines and rules for His followers to live an abundant life, are found in the Sermon on the Mount. This sermon includes most of His fundamental truths. **We will focus on four of them in this and the following three chapters: the Golden Rule, the Beatitudes, the Lord's Prayer, and Salt and Light.**

Snapshot Picture of Scripture (Matthew 5, 6, 7; 7:12)

The Sermon on the Mount is found only in the gospel of Matthew (a Jew and former tax collector) in chapters five, six, and seven. Notice that except for the first two and last two verses there is no narrative included in these three consecutive chapters—only the continuous words of Jesus. Most Biblical scholars agree the Sermon on the Mount was taught over a period of several days, but the exact number is not recorded.

The actual words 'Sermon on the Mount' are not found in the original scriptures. They were later added by Bible scholars and translators for clearer reading and understanding.

The title was based on the two verses right before He started teaching. "Now when Jesus saw the crowds, he went up on a mountainside and sat down. His disciples came to him, and he began to teach them" (Matthew 5:1-2 NIV).

This sermon is considered a kind of manifesto describing how life should be in God's kingdom. It takes some of the familiar Mosaic laws and broadens their applications to demonstrate faith in God and loving others. *The phrase 'Kingdom of Heaven' appears 33 times and 'Kingdom of God' four times.*

It took place toward the beginning of Jesus' earthly ministry. It followed His baptism by John the Baptist, being tested in the wilderness, and calling His first disciples.

His message covered many topics including: Love for Enemies, Giving to the Needy, Prayer, Worry, and Judging Others. When He finished His sermon, the audience was mesmerized by what they'd heard. "When Jesus had finished saying these things, the crowds were amazed at his teaching, because he taught as one who had authority, and not as their teachers of the law" (Matthew 7:28-29 NIV).

A gold nugget found in the middle of the stream.

Almost hidden in the middle of the last chapter, under His teaching about asking, seeking, and knocking, we find one of the most universal familiar principles of His message commonly known as The Golden Rule. This title began to be linked to this life-lesson of Jesus during the 16th-17th centuries.

"So in everything, do to others what you would have them do to you, for this sums up the Law and the Prophets" (Matthew 7:12 NIV).

In this one verse Jesus brilliantly condenses the entire Old

Testament into this single principle. It gives us a standard by which we can gauge our actions—actively treat others the way we want to be treated.

Everyone wants to be shown love, respect, and appreciation. If you want to receive a smile or kind words from others, then smile and speak kindly to them. If you want to be helped in times of need, then help others when they are struggling.

Interestingly, some critics say it is a common principle shared by other religions. But Jesus' command has a subtle but very important difference.

- **Buddhism:** "Hurt not others…"
- **Hinduism:** "This is the sum of duty: do not do to others…"
- **Confucianism:** "Do not do to others…"

The Eastern Religions state negatively and passively to 'refrain from doing'. Jesus says positively to 'look for ways to actively show love'.

Take a step or walk a while in someone's shoes.

"Walk a mile in someone's shoes" is attributed to Native American tribes and a poem by Mary Lathrap *Judge Softly* which ends with the closing line, "Take the time to walk a mile in his moccasins."

It is further emphasized in the Sermon on the Mount when Jesus points out we should not only take action to help others but be willing to do more than they ask or need. "If anyone asks you to go one mile, go with them two miles" (Matthew 5:41 NIV).

This principle of taking action begins with a non-judgmental empathetic mindset. Empathy is a respectful understanding of what others are experiencing. It helps us to live by the Golden Rule by imagining how we would like to be treated if we were experiencing what they are. *What would be your reaction if you were a passenger on a bus in the following story?*

The Man On A Bus.

It was a typical, restful Saturday afternoon on a bus. People were sitting quietly–some reading newspapers, some lost in thought, some resting with their eyes closed. It was a calm, peaceful scene.

Then suddenly a man and his four children brashly entered the bus. The children were so loud and rambunctious that instantly the whole climate changed.

The man sat down and closed his eyes, apparently oblivious to the situation. The children were yelling back and forth, throwing things, even grabbing people's papers. It was disturbing and irritating, and yet, the man did nothing.

The lady sitting beside him couldn't take it any longer and finally turned and said, "Sir, your children are really disturbing a lot of people. Can you please try to control them a little more?"

The man lifted his gaze as if to come to a consciousness of the situation and said softly, "Oh, you're right. I'm sorry. I guess I should do something about it. You see, we just came from the hospital where their mother died a few hours ago. I don't know what to think or do and I guess they don't know how to handle it either."

The lady sitting next to the man immediately thought and felt differently. Her irritation vanished and her heart was filled with the man's pain. Feelings of empathy and compassion flowed freely.

Demonstrating how we show and share love to others begins with a mindset of walking in their shoes and treating them with kindness and love with which we would like to be treated!

Positive Points to Ponder

- Beginning today, treat everyone you meet as if this will be their last day on earth. Show all the care, kindness and love you can and your life will never be the same.
- Before you abuse, criticize, or accuse, please take the time to walk a mile in their shoes.

35

8 Ways to Be Blessed in a Mess

A law was passed in a country which prohibited the public use of the word God or *divine being*—any word or phrase that even implied a religious or spiritual reference at public gatherings.

As the students at a local high school proceeded through their graduation program all the speeches by class leaders were very touching. Dads fought wet eyes as moms wiped freely flowing tears with tissues. But something just did not seem right. Everyone missed the opening convocation prayer and the tradition of the graduates being blessed by a local minister.

Then everyone quietly watched a single, solitary student walk to the microphone on stage and raise both arms in the air. When he brought them down everyone in the graduating class did the strangest thing. They all sneezed! That's right. They sneezed at the exact same time.

But what happened next was amazing. The student looked at his classmates, smiled and proudly yelled, "God Bless You!" What followed was a thunderous, five-minute standing ovation!

There are a number of words frequently used in a believer's vocabulary but one heard quite often is *blessed*. "Bless you", "Have a blessed day," and in our part of the county it's not unusual to hear someone say, "Bless his little heart." But what does blessed really mean?

The Greek word most often translated as "blessed" means "happy." And it doesn't utilize an abundance of brain cells to recall some familiar phrases including *happy:* Happy go lucky, Don't worry be happy, As happy as a lark, A happy camper, Strike a happy medium, One big happy family, Happy Birthday, Happy New Year, and Happy Holidays.

But the biblical meaning of blessed is much deeper and more meaningful than our typical reference to a state of being happy. Perhaps the most familiar use of *blessed* in the Bible is found in the Beatitudes. It is used to describe an outcome of following Christ as deep, joy-filled contentment. *To be truly blessed is to experience the full impact of God's love, peace, power, promises and presence in our lives!*

In each beatitude Jesus describes a Christian character trait and then shares the result of trusting in Him and believing nothing can separate us from His love—regardless of the circumstance.

It is interesting that many during Jesus' ministry considered Him the new Moses but there are explicit differences.

Moses ascended, then came down from the mountain and stood—Jesus went up to the mountain and sat down. God spoke to Moses with thunder and lightning—Jesus speaks in a still, small voice. People were told to keep their distance from Moses—Jesus invites us to draw near. People could keep the Mosaic laws and not change—Jesus gives us a choice and tells us we will be changed!

The following Beatitudes describe the ideal disciple and her/his reward, both present and future. Jesus has recently started His ministry, is becoming extremely popular, and huge crowds are following Him. He is sitting on what is now called the Mount of Beatitudes in Galilee and begins teaching these words to hundreds of His followers.

Snapshot Picture of Scripture (Matthew 5:3-10 NKJV)

"Blessed are the poor in spirit, For theirs is the kingdom of heaven." God blesses those who humbly realize that all their blessings in life come from Him.

"Blessed are those who mourn, For they shall be comforted." God blesses those who are truly sorry for their sins and are comforted knowing their troubles in this life are only temporary.

"Blessed are the meek, For they shall inherit the earth." God blesses those who are considerate and submissive to His will, and they will eventually inherit eternal riches.

"Blessed are those who hunger and thirst for righteousness, For they shall be filled." God blesses those who are spiritually hungry and thirsty for Him and His Word and they will be filled with love that lasts forever.

"Blessed are the merciful, For they shall obtain mercy." This alludes to the Golden Rule reminding us that God blesses those who show mercy, compassion, love and forgiveness and they will be shown the same.

"Blessed are the pure in heart, For they shall see God." God blesses those who strive to exemplify love and humility in everything they do, and He will reveal himself to them.

"Blessed are the peacemakers, For they shall be called sons of God." God blesses those who seek eternal peace that only He offers, and they will become one of His children.

"Blessed are those who are persecuted for righteousness' sake, For theirs is the kingdom of heaven." God blesses those who may be treated badly and unfairly–physically or emotionally–because they hold true to their faith and will be blessed in the next life.

True Story of being 'Blessed in A Mess'.

Every day after work Mary gathered her spare change and put it aside to give to the homeless man standing at the exit of the highway. She quickly rolled down her window and handed him the coins. Occasionally, the light would turn red, and they would ask each other about their day.

His answer would always be the same. *"Thank God I am blessed."* It amazed her that even in his situation he was so positive, and it reminded her of how blessed she was.

Then one day she was called into her boss's office and told she would be laid off. Shocked and upset, all she could think about the rest of the day was how she was going to provide for her family and pay her bills.

Needless to say, Mary didn't think about gathering her coins for the homeless man until she saw him. She hoped she would catch the light green but missed it. As she waited for the light to change, he strolled over to her car.

He greeted her with his usual smile, and when she rolled down the window, he did something that blew her away. As he reached in his pocket he said, "Today I want to give *you* a dollar." Mary burst into tears, and if the light hadn't turned green, she would have jumped out of the car and hugged him.

Understand that he gave her more than a dollar bill—he taught her a valuable life lesson. No matter how bad life seems (like losing her job with no savings) she thought, *"Even in this mess, thank God I am blessed!"*

A summary of being blessed in a mess with joy and happiness.

Live a life showing and sharing God's kindness, love, and compassion to others. Be humble and don't take yourself too seriously. Be grateful for all you have. Trust God and rely on His strength and you will be happier with a deeper sense of joy than you can possibly imagine—now and forever!

Positive Points to Ponder
- Blessed and happy are those with hearts that bend for they will never be broken, and the hearts that are cracked for they will let in light.
- The Garden of Eden was man's original Happy Place. If there is anyone who should be truly happy and joyful and filled with laughter it is Christians.

36

Pray This–Not That

As a teen I attended a week-long series of services each summer at our denomination's retreat center called 'Camp Meeting'. It was held in an old-fashioned tabernacle that was open on all sides, had wood shavings on the floor and hard, uncomfortable chairs that were guaranteed to make your back ache until the next morning.

Most of the campers were adults, so a small group of us teens were there to 'serve others' during the day by playing ball and going swimming. But we were required to attend the marathon nightly services.

It was commonly expected that the evangelists' prayers and sermons would be lengthy but one summer the time of the featured preacher's oratory was unprecedented. His pre-sermon prayers were about a third as long as his over-one-hour sermons.

We teens were so impressed that we started timing his prayers. (One of the ministers attending told us in confidence that if that's the worst thing we did it was understandable and forgivable. In fact, he found it a real challenge to stay focused himself.)

The speaker's prayers became longer each night and by the final service we could hardly contain ourselves but had no choice since we were in a spiritual service. On the last night, he broke the all-time camp meeting record as his prayer lasted 23 minutes and 17 seconds!

I will be the first to admit that I don't spend nearly enough time in prayer, but there is a time and a place for everything. It may be unnecessary to pray for every missionary in 17 countries by name when the purpose of the prayer is simply to ask the Lord's blessing on a sermon.

Obviously he missed the memo regarding research that states the average time an adult can focus on one topic is 17 minutes. And for teens, let's not even go there.

In the Sermon On the Mount, Jesus shared a prayer that serves as a model or pattern for His followers that began with His words, "This, then, is how you should pray."

Snapshot Picture of Scripture (Matthew 6:9-13 NKJV)
"Our Father in heaven" is telling us whom to pray to—our Father. "Hallowed be your name" emphasizes that we are to worship and praise God. The verse "Your kingdom come, Your will be done on earth as it is in heaven" focuses on praying for God's will in our lives.

"Give us this day our daily bread" means to ask God for our daily *needs*, not wants or desires. "And forgive us our debts, as we forgive our debtors" reminds us to forgive others as God forgave us.

The last verse of the prayer is a request to help us overcome temptation and to protect us from the evil one. "And do not lead us into temptation but deliver us from the evil one. "For Yours is the kingdom and the power and the glory forever. Amen"

Note: Many times, Jews added a praise or doxology to the end of a prayer, and this last part of verse 13 is absent in many original manuscripts and modern Bible translations.

Some people treat the Lord's Prayer as a magic formula as if the words themselves have some specific influence with God. But Jesus introduced a revolutionary idea that we are to pray from our hearts, not just recite the same memorized words.

As a pastor I would often remind our congregation to think about what we are saying and, "Don't just say it–really pray it." There is nothing wrong with memorizing the prayer, but we should mean the words we say.

Power-Packed Principles Pertaining to Prayer
God is never in a hurry. In some countries, when you're a guest and the host fills your glass, it means you are welcome here. And when he fills your glass to overflowing, it means he never wants you to leave, and he will stay with you as long as you are there.

It is easy to think God is so important we feel like we need to be brief and pray a short prayer. But God is never looking at his watch or phone to see what time it is or has something else to do.

He is never looking over your shoulder because there is someone else with whom he would rather be having a conversation. You never need to worry about overstaying your welcome. When you are in the presence of the King and your cup overflows, he doesn't want you to leave.

Most Important...Prayer or Bible Study? Someone asked the great English preacher, Charles Spurgeon, which was most important, prayer or Bible study? He responded with a question, "Which is more important, inhaling or exhaling?"

He continued by sharing that we need both. Inhale the Word of God. Exhale prayer. God tells us to abide in Him and He will abide in us. (John 15:4-9)

Gratitude for Divine Delays or Divine Detours. The rules of football include a penalty for a 'delay of game'. Sometimes God delays an answer to our prayers. But it's actually just a *Devine Detour*. If we always receive the answer when we want it, we may not be prepared for it.

Be grateful and thank God for the delays, detours, redirections, and closed doors. Thank Him for being a caring Father who doesn't always give us what we want when we want it, but out of His perfect love gives us more than we need.

God Gave Me What I Asked For

I asked for strength and God gave me difficulties to make me strong.
I asked for wisdom and God gave me problems to solve.
I asked for courage and God gave me dangers to overcome.
I asked for love and God gave me troubled people to help.
All my prayers were answered.
God gave me exactly what I asked for!

Prayer changes things. My dad had a plaque on his wall that read, "Prayer Changes Things." That is certainly true. But we have a tendency to assume that when we don't see changes in our circumstances, we may sometimes conclude that God is not working.

When you pray, something is always accomplished. During every moment spent in prayer, *you* are changing. During every moment *you* are growing. During every moment your character is becoming more like Christ. Whether you see it or feel it or not, prayer is doing something–it is changing YOU!

Prayers don't have an expiration date. One of the most repulsive things to me is the smell or taste of soured milk after the expiration date. It tells me it is no longer useful.

The march around Jericho proves prayers don't expire. The

Israelites believed when they prayed, "The wall will fall." They thought of *problem solving* as *prayer solving*. Pray expectantly and believe it can and will happen. *Share a prayer with urgent care!*

Prayer is a two-way street. Most late-night television talk show hosts begin by sharing a monologue. They do all the talking and the audience listens.

Prayer is a *dialogue*. It is simply a conversation with God. Most of us do a lot more talking than listening when we pray. That's one reason Jesus taught us to distance ourselves from distractions of our world and find a private place to pray. The classic instruction from elementary school when crossing the street applies to prayer. Stop, look, and *listen*.

Pray consistently. The longest time I recall going without food is two days and that was only because I was ill. On a daily basis I'm guilty of eating way more than three times a day. What if we prayed daily as often as we ate?

Daniel's motto for praying must have been something like, "Stop, Drop and Pray." Even when a law was passed restricting prayer he went to his room, opened a window, and prayed at least three times a day–every day.

When to pray. In addition to specific quiet times set aside to pray, express the desires of your heart and listen. *Morning*: Before your feet hit the floor give thanks. David says, "In the morning, O Lord, you will hear my voice" (Psalm 5:3 NIV). *During the Day*: Take 'breath prayers'. Pause and express gratitude and needs. *Night*: Before 'lights out' reflect on a blessing from your day.

A child's prayer from the heart can teach us how to start.

A mother stood outside her young daughter's slightly opened bedroom door one night watching and listening to her recite the ABC's as she knelt beside her bed. When finished she asked her daughter what she was doing.

When the little girl shared that she was praying, the mother asked why she was reciting the alphabet. The young girl explained, "Well, I don't know the right words to pray, and I know God is really smart. So, I just say the letters of the alphabet and believe that God will put the letters together in the right order to make the words I'm trying to say."

That sums up the entire lesson Christ taught about praying. **Pray**

from your heart and truly believe God will do His part!

Positive Points to Ponder
- God is bigger than any law. They may not be shared on the PA system, but as long as there are tests and exams, there will always be prayer in schools.
- Always pray to have: eyes that see the best in people; a heart that forgives the worst; a mind that forgets the bad; and a soul that never loses faith in God!

37

The Salt Tastes Right and You Are the Light

As a result of the Cold War and the identification of spies from foreign countries in the early 1960's, the Federal Civil Defense Administration recommended that in case of a nuclear war families should build a Fallout Shelter near their home.

Some of the emergency recommendations included: build a 10 x 12 foot underground concrete room with a door that can be sealed, stock with an adequate supply of food and water to last two weeks, a transistor radio, and artificial lighting with batteries.

Fortunately, they never had to be used for the purpose with which they were built. But when our family moved to a rental house that had an underground Fallout Shelter in the backyard, my fourth-grade friends and I found an alternate use that was way more fun than the original plan. It was the perfect place to hold the secret weekly meetings of our "Basement Backyard Boy's Club."

That is until one day when 'the lights went out in Georgia'—actually, it was South Carolina. In our laughter and discussing the 'agenda' for the meeting we failed to realize that our only flashlight was slowly dimming until it eventually stopped working.

We found ourselves in the deepest depth of darkness I've ever experienced. With absolutely no light it was impossible to see anything or anyone. We started to crawl on our hands and knees while feeling our way up the concrete steps. But when we attempted to push the ground-level door open, we realized we had forgotten our usual ritual of slightly propping it open with a rock. No matter how hard we pushed, the heavy door would not budge.

After yelling, screaming, a little crying, and beating on the door for what seemed like ages–more than likely about twenty minutes, the door suddenly opened. The light almost blinded us but was a welcome sight. We were even happy to hear the words of the lady opening it, whom we referred to as 'Nancy the Nosy Neighbor,' as she asked, "What in the world are you boys doing down there?"

One of the most life-changing lessons Jesus shared in the Sermon on the Mount was that His followers are to be the light in a world of darkness.

Snapshot Picture of Scripture (Matthew 5:14-16 NKJV)
"You are the light of the world. A city that is set on a hill cannot be hidden. Nor do they light a lamp and put it under a basket, but on a lampstand, and it gives light to all who are in the house. Let your light so shine before men, that they may see your good works and glorify your Father in heaven."

A reminder that Jesus is sharing these words with a huge crowd, many of whom are hearing His message for the first time. So, the Master Teacher uses familiar objects such as a lamp, basket, and a lampstand as spiritual analogies to help them understand.

During the life of Christ, almost every Jewish home had at least one important piece of furniture–a lampstand. It was usually a tall pedestal with one main shaft that branched out at the top, holding more than one candle. And if a person covered the candles with a vessel such as a bowl or basket, no one would be able to see the light.

Light is to be revealed and not concealed.
We can let our light shine to others by offering love and forgiveness and sharing the Good News. We can take time to listen to someone during a tough season of their life, donate to a worthy cause, or humbly and compassionately serve those who can't repay us.

I recently visited Chris and went with Malachi and him on his weekly mission. Every weekend, regardless of the weather, he loads his gas grill, takes it to a local park, and cooks breakfast for the homeless.

Several years ago, I was riding with Jon near his home when he unexpectedly parked his SUV on the side of a street. As he opened his back door, homeless people gathered to receive a snack and water that he always carries with him.

Both Chris and Jon reminded me by their actions that letting God's light shine in a dark world is many times unseen by others and is helping the helpless without expecting anything in return.

C. S. Lewis said, "Don't shine so that others can see you. Shine so that through you, others can see Him."

Share Your Light

If a flashlight slowly grows dim or stops shining, you don't throw it away. You just change the batteries. If a friend is in a dark place in their life, you don't ignore them. You help them change their batteries.

Some need and an 'A'=Attention
Some need an 'AA'=Attention and Affection
Some need an 'AAA'=Attention, Affection and Acceptance
Some need a 'C'=Compassion
Some need a 'D'=Direction

And if they still don't seem to shine? Simply sit with them quietly and share *your* light!

What about the salt?

In addition to light, Jesus taught in the previous verse we are also to be salt.

Salt had two purposes in the Middle East of the first century. Because of the lack of refrigeration, salt was used to preserve food, especially meat. And as it does now, it was used as a flavor enhancer. It may not be recommended for a healthy diet, but just the right amount of salt brings out the flavor in food.

I clearly recall walking into the Ham House on my Granddad King's farm. It was a small building filled with hams hanging on poles that were cured by salt or smoke. It won't be found today on any doctor's recommended nutrition programs, but one of my favorite meats is 'country ham'.

In Colossians Paul tells us to 'let our words be seasoned with salt'. *We are encouraged to show how the Good News has impacted our conversations positively as we bring a different "flavor" and try to build others up with encouraging words.*

Positive Points to Ponder

- We should not ask, "What is wrong with the world?" Rather, we should ask ourselves, "How can I be a tastier salt and a brighter light?"

- **Jesus Is the Light of the World**

Which means He is the Light of YOUR world.
> The Light in your darkness
> your marriage, your children,
> your depression, your fears,
> your hardest moments,
> your biggest mountains, and
> your greatest disappointments,
> He is the Light of YOUR world!

Section 3: GAME TIME!

You have learned life lessons and strategies regarding how to deal with situations and challenges. You've reviewed the basic instructions needed to find hope and joy and how to be inspired to light your faith-fire.

Now it's time to stop talking and start walking. Time to put it all together and start living by giving. Time to stop being just a fan in the stands and start being a follower who makes a real difference in the lives of the people in *your* world.

These last three chapters contain some of our most valuable life-changing lessons.

38. "Trust the Son of Man With Your Life-Plan"
39. "Find Jubilant Joy in Your Journey"
40. "Unleash Unlimited Love and Start Living Life Out Loud!"

LET'S GO!

38

Trust the Son of Man for Your Life-Plan

I recently read that *most people spend more time planning their vacations than planning their life*. It intrigued me to reflect on some of life's many experiences for which we make plans:
- Graduation Plans
- Wedding Plans
- Emergency Plans
- Health/Fitness Plans
- Financial Plans
- Retirement Plans

Having a good plan can result in a life that is more blessed and less of a mess. The key word in that statement is '*good* plan'.

I heard a story about a man who thought he had a fool-proof plan for sneaking into a drive-in movie without paying. If you are unfamiliar, a drive-in movie is a form of entertainment where people sit in their vehicle, hook an external speaker on their window, and watch the movie on a huge screen through their windshield.

He planned to crawl into the trunk of his car before arriving and his wife would pay only for herself. Once inside, she would let him out of the trunk. The plan sounded good, but it failed.

In former years separate keys were used for the ignition and the trunk. When she tried to open the trunk, they realized he had the trunk key in his pocket—inside the trunk. Hours later after the firemen cut through the trunk, he finally crawled out. In addition to being embarrassed, they didn't get to watch the movie for which she paid. Some plans sound good but simply don't work.

A guy in the Old Testament named Joseph is a great example of determination to be faithful and follow God's plan for his life, even when it didn't make sense. He didn't know the outcome and there were multiple bumps along the way. As you read the plot of this true and fascinating story, you may agree that it would make a phenomenal action movie.

Snapshot Picture of Scripture (Genesis 37-50)

Joseph was the eleventh son of Jacob. Jacob admittedly loved Joseph more than any of his other sons. His brothers were obviously jealous and angry and devised a plan to kill him.

But his oldest brother, Reuben, suggested they instead throw him in a well. They dipped his favorite robe in goat's blood and told their father he had been killed by wild animals. His brothers then sold him to a high-ranking Egyptian, and he eventually became supervisor of his household.

After being falsely accused of rape and thrown in prison, Joseph was later called to interpret the king's troubling dreams, and when his prediction became reality, he became a ruler in Egypt. He was put in charge of storing up food and selling it during the coming famine.

When famine struck the land, his father Jacob sent his brothers to Egypt to buy grain. At first, they didn't recognize Joseph, but he recognized them. When they eventually realized who he was, in spite of how they treated him, he forgave them. Joseph shared one of the most profound statements of the story, "You intended to harm me, but God intended it for good to accomplish what is now being done" (Genesis 50:20 NIV).

Joseph sent his brothers back home to retrieve their father Jacob and the remainder of their families so he could provide for them. They lived in Egypt for 400 years and when Moses led the Hebrews out of Egypt, he took the remains of Joseph with him as Joseph had requested.

Divine Detours, Delays and Disappointments

Recently I was driving in a nearby familiar city but because of the 'Road Under Construction' signs, I had to take a detour. My original planned route was simple, but because of driving in an unfamiliar area with poorly marked signs and the alternate route undetected on my GPS, the trip became a real challenge.

Even though Joseph had a vision of his life's destination, he had no idea the plan God had prepared for him or where that plan would cause him to arrive. Similarly, sometimes we are required to take a spiritual Divine Detour or Delay with disappointments along the way of which we had not planned.

When our plans tend to lead us in the wrong direction, or possibly to a Dead End, it doesn't necessarily mean we made a wrong turn or decision. Actually, it may be so God's plan can work and may turn out to be our biggest blessings.

It is easy to think only the good things that happen in your life are a part of God's plan. But it's also the disappointments, the closed doors, and the people who treat us badly–like Joseph's brothers. Trust God's process and plans, and don't see the negative things as hindrances but a necessary part of His plan for us to become who He wants us to be.

God has a specific life-plan for YOU!

God has a *general plan* for everyone that includes establishing and developing a personal relationship with Him through His Son.

He also designed a *personal plan* for believers. As you obey His general plan you will discover His uniquely designed individual plan for you. His plan unfolds naturally in baby-steps and small segments at a time as we grow in faith. His plan for you may look different in different seasons of your life.

- Use your talents, abilities, gifts, and opportunities to serve Him through others in your unique ways where you are right now.
- Daily share and show God's love through your actions.
- Make a habit of praying, reading His Word and finding a place of worship to fellowship and grow with other believers.
- The most simple and meaningful advice: 'Trust and Obey'!

Sometimes we make finding God's plan for us more complicated than it needs to be. "'For I know the plans I have for you,' declares the Lord, 'plans to prosper you and not to harm you, plans to give you hope and a future'" (Jeremiah 29:11 NIV).

God sometimes incubates greatness in ordinary people like you in small places, in tight places, in isolated places. He may hold you back until everything is ready and *you* are ready. And then–BOOM! He will open the door for you and say, "Come on down." *When your life is in chaos or crisis remember that He has a plan!*

Building plans for your future.

A carpenter of thirty years told his boss he was retiring. His boss asked him to build one more house. He agreed but his heart wasn't in the project, so he put in less effort, cut corners, and used inferior materials.

When he finished, his boss handed him the keys and told him the house was his retirement gift for all his dedicated years. The carpenter was shocked and disappointed in himself for not following his usual plans and effort. *Don't build your life without seeking God's plan for you.*

Don't try to figure out His plan by yourself. "Trust in the LORD with all your heart, and do not lean on your own understanding. In all your ways submit to Him, and He will make your paths straight" (Proverbs 3:5-6 NIV).

Sometimes we see limitations, but God sees opportunities. We see faults, but God sees growth. We see problems, but God sees solutions. We see only this life, but God sees eternity.

Thankfully, God's plans for us are always better than ours. Pray for a vision and direction to follow His plan, patience to wait on it, and the wisdom to know when it comes.

My personal plan.

With only a few weeks left before my official retirement as a school administrator, Lucy and I visited Snowville Christian Church–a beautiful, rural church about ten miles from our home. Unknown to us, the church did not have a pastor and when they learned that I filled in for ministers for Sunday morning worship services, I received a call to share a message a couple of weeks later.

The next week I received a phone call and an invitation to their board meeting to get to know each other, share my spiritual beliefs and leadership experience, and to possibly be considered as their next pastor. As an obvious example of Divine Intervention or a Godwink, I retired as an educator on June 30 and on August 1 became the pastor of one of the most loving, caring church families I've been blessed to be a part of!

I am certainly not predicting that God's plan for your life will include a change in your job or career. There is a good possibility He wants you to 'Bloom Where You Are Planted'. But I can personally and passionately encourage you that whatever He has in your plan, remember: *God may take you in directions you didn't know you needed in order to bring you more than you could ever imagine.*

Trust the Son of Man with Your Life-Plan!

Positive Points to Ponder
- God has already prepared a plan—now He's preparing YOU!
- He may want you to remain where you are. But your current situation may or may not be your final destination. Certain things may need to end so greater things can begin!

39

Find Jubilant Joy on Your Life-Journey

It's 4:30 a.m. and our car is packed for the family trip from Virginia to Florida. We are leaving early hoping to get a few miles and hours behind us before Jon and Chris wake up.

In the morning darkness I quietly carry them to the car. After less than five minutes on the road, we are at the edge of town when—WHAM!

"What was that?" Lucy frantically asked as both boys immediately awakened and sat up. We all watched in disbelief as a huge deer tumbled in front of the car then quickly got to his feet, ran up a nearby bank, and disappeared into the woods.

We are all now fully awake and trying to figure out where the deer came from and how it appeared so quickly. Our original plans for the rejuvenating journey to the Sunshine State are now gone. And before long we find ourselves trying to solve the problem of opening the hood with a bent release handle in the front grill—compliments of the deer that did the distressing damage.

Perhaps you've experienced some unexpected surprises during your life-journey. Experiences that seemingly created the farthest thing from *joy*. We can learn invaluable insights on how to 'Find Jubilant Joy in Your Life-Journey' by reading the words of the Apostle Paul.

Snapshot Picture of Scripture (Philippians 1-4)

As we review some of Paul's wise words of wisdom about living a joyful life in an unhappy world, be reminded of who he was, what he did, and from where he wrote some of his letters.

A reminder that prior to becoming a follower of Christ, Paul was a devout Jew who sincerely believed God's plan for his life was to persecute and terrorize Christians. He held the clothes of Stephen—the first Christian martyr—as people stoned him to death. Understandably, Christians stayed away from Paul as he was not a nice guy to hang out with.

But that drastically changed when he was dramatically converted on the road to Damascus and became a phenomenal follower of Jesus. (Acts 9). He is credited with eventually writing 13 of the 27 books in the New Testament! One of those books—written to the Philippians—is known as the 'Joy Letter'. *In only four chapters, he uses the words joy or rejoicing 17 times.* As you read some of his encouraging words, keep in mind he wrote from a prison in Rome as he possibly anticipated his execution.

"In all my prayers for all of you, I always pray with joy" (Philippians 1:4 NIV). Pray with *joy*, really? If I was writing a letter from prison, there's a good possibility I'd be complaining about the cold floor I'm sleeping on, the bad food, or the guy in the next cell who snores too loudly. The Philippians' acts of kindness made him think of them with joy. *Focus on God's blessings, not on our burdens.*

"I am glad and rejoice with all of you. So, you too should be glad and rejoice with me" (Philippians 2:17b-18 NIV). Unity and working together with other believers are an important part of living a joyful life.

"Rejoice in the Lord always; again, I will say, rejoice" (Philippians 4:4 NIV). As Paul nears the end of his letter, he focuses on the importance of being joyful during our journey. It is so important to rejoice he shares twice in the same verse. *And He doesn't instruct us to rejoice some of the time or most of the time, but 'always'.*

Again, visualize where he is located while writing about joy. He is not lounging in a beach chair on a Caribbean Island with a gentle ocean breeze blowing while sipping a refreshing Bahama Mama beverage. He is sharing joy and happiness from prison!

Joy is an inside job.

Joy is different from happiness as it is not based on a temporary situation but begins with a change in our heart. This doesn't mean feeling happy is not important. In 1979 McDonalds added what became one of the most popular and successful menu items in the history of the fast-food business: Happy Meals. But being 'happy' lasted only until the customer ate the last french fry.

We should enjoy special happy times while understanding that it is joy, based on our relationship with Christ, that is eternal—regardless of our current circumstances.

Someone has stated:
> If you want to be happy for an hour, enjoy a delicious meal.
> If you want to be happy for a day, play golf or go shopping.
> If you want to be happy for a week, go on a vacation.
> But if you want to be full of happiness and joy for your life-journey, faithfully follow Christ!

Facing challenges with joy on your journey.

It was this deep joy from his heart that enabled Paul to overcome hardships during his three major missionary journeys. He endured persecution, shipwreck, prison, beatings, stoning, falsely accused of starting a riot, and personal health challenges.

Paul describes his health or physical challenge as a 'thorn in my flesh' which caused great pain and discomfort. Scholars have speculated but most admit we don't know exactly what his physical challenge was.

A personal perspective: Perhaps like me and others, this is the only challenge he faced with which we can personally relate. I have experienced Autoimmune Hepatitis–an irreversible and incurable liver disease, for over 20 years.

On the very first day I started typing the manuscript for this book, I took a break for a doctor appointment to learn the results of recent blood tests. I was literally shocked when my doctor shared that I had cancer, and because of the AIH and an extremely low immune system, the doctors' first recommendation of surgery was not an option. Even though there would possibly be complications, thankfully I could undergo radiation treatments.

Isn't God's timing interesting–and sometimes almost humorous? I'm writing a book titled, *Good News You Can Use* only to receive, seemingly at the time, some of the worst news of my life.

Perhaps your personal hardships include losing a job, grieving a friend or family member, a relationship that couldn't be rescued, financial challenges, or an abusive situation.

By following Paul's example of how to maintain joy during detours or disappointments in our own journey, he shares what the Lord said to him. "My grace is all you need. My power works best in weakness" (2 Corinthians 12:9 NLT).

You're never alone on your journey. Solomon tells us to, "Trust in the Lord with all your heart and lean not on your own understanding. In all your ways acknowledge him and he will direct your paths" (Proverbs 3:5-6 NIV).

He was also saying *you don't need to figure it out by yourself.* Your heart can be deceitful. Your emotions fluctuate. Your understanding doesn't see the whole picture. But God never changes, never lies, and knows everything. So, trust your Heavenly Father.

Even if you are not sure how it is going to work out, keep prayerfully taking the steps that God is showing you. Let him guide you because even though the path might be unknown to you, God is the One that laid it ahead of you. *He knows and He's got you!*

True stories say it best.

In the 1992 Olympics, Derek Redmond pulled a hamstring but was determined to finish the race. After he collapsed his father, Jim, rushed to the track, held up his son, and shared they would finish the race together.

That's how compassionate our Heavenly Father is. When we fall on our journey, He is there to pick us up and carry us.

A financially successful man was driving his very expensive car down a street when he saw a little boy throw a brick that hit his car. He immediately stopped the car, jumped out, and while screaming at the boy asked why in the world he would do such a terrible thing.

The little boy apologized, and with tears rolling down his cheeks, explained that his younger brother was crippled and fell out of his wheelchair at the curb, and he couldn't pick him up. Crushed with empathy and compassion the man carried the boy's brother to his car, loaded his wheelchair, and gave them both a ride home.

By the way, the man never had the dent repaired. He left it as a daily self-reminder not to go through life's journey so fast someone has to throw a brick to get his attention. *Sometimes God may slow us down so we can help someone on their journey or so the danger that's waiting on us will pass.*

Sheep follow the Shepherd for a safe and joyful journey!

A familiar parable is told when a shepherd leaves the 99 sheep to find the one that is lost. One of the points of the story is that Jesus loves us so much He will leave everything until He finds us and carries us home.

But have you ever thought about what the sheep may have thought on the night Christ was born? After the angel disappeared, the shepherds left the 99 and began a journey to find *the One*? The sheep must have wondered 'what is this about'?

The shepherds went on a journey, not to seek the lost one, but the *One* who is never lost. Not the one who wanders through creation, but the *One* who is the Wonder of Creation. Not the one who needs to be saved, but the *One* who came to save. *We should never stop our journey seeking the One!*

Jesus invited a bunch of fishermen to be followers and go on a journey with Him. Ordinary people like you and me. He didn't say, "Follow me and suddenly your life will be perfect." Or "I've been searching everywhere and you're just about the most holy people I could find."

It was simple. It *is* simple. The key that unlocks the door to begin your journey is to simply follow. He doesn't say it will be a walk in the park. Or whether the walk will be long or short. This journey is going from walking alone to walking with Jesus.

Christ reminds us about finding joy on our journey. "I have told you these things that you might be filled with joy. Yes, your joy will overflow" (John 15:11 NLT).

As you prepare your heart for our last chapter, my prayer is that in your life-journey you will be safe and enjoy the ride. *Remember when you lose your way and are lost, God is always waiting for you with open arms to joyfully welcome you back home!*

Positive Points to Ponder
- God never said the journey would be easy, but He did say the destination would be better than you can ever imagine!
- Life is a journey that sometimes includes pitstops, flat tires, and running on an empty tank. So joyfully live your best today and God will take you where you need to be tomorrow!

40

Unleash Unlimited Love and Start Living Life Out Loud!

As the keynote speaker, I'm sitting on the stage of historic Burruss Hall Auditorium on the Virginia Tech campus looking at a capacity standing-room-only crowd of over 3,000 people. Long lines extended beside both walls from the front to the rear with people holding cameras waiting to video or take a picture of this special occasion. I could feel the excitement and anticipation while everyone waited for the program to begin.

This auditorium was personally meaningful as through the years I attended many concerts and heard nationally recognized speakers.

If you tend to be even slightly impressed with the above description–don't be. The reality is not a single person in the audience came to hear me speak.

I was invited to speak at the graduation of my alma mater, Blacksburg High School. I'm certain they could hardly wait for me to finish speaking so the celebration could begin for the real reason everyone was present–to receive their diploma.

And I completely understand that by the next morning most of the audience had likely forgotten 99 percent of what I shared. In fact, I only vaguely recall one statement–and I was the speaker.

It went something like, "As you go into the real world, remember that relationships and showing kindness and love to others are some of the most important things in life." So much for my life-changing words of wisdom.

As we begin this final chapter about the Good News, it is crucial to look at the last instructions Jesus shared with His followers—then and now. He is basically telling us that, 'of all the lessons and stories I've taught and all the things you've seen Me do, *these* are the things I want you to remember, and *this* is what I want you to do after I'm gone'.

Snapshot Picture of Scripture (Luke 8-10)

Jesus' last instructions before leaving earth can be found in all four gospels. When we read Luke 8-10 one instruction consisting of one simple, but powerful word really stands out–*Go*. In these three chapters He tells His followers four times to *Go*. *That one word is mentioned in the Bible 1,542 times!*

A man Jesus healed wanted to go with Him but was instead told to go home and share what had happened. Jesus knew that everyone was aware of the man's condition, and he would be a powerful witness of what He had done. He instructed him to 'go back to his family and tell them everything God had done for him'.

Luke records that Jesus later tells another man who wanted to follow Him to 'go and proclaim the Kingdom of God'.

Far more than just the 12 disciples were following Jesus. He eventually designated a group of 72 and reminded them that when and where they go, they would face opposition.

And after sharing with an expert in the law the parable of the Good Samaritan and explaining what loving his neighbor really looks like, Jesus told him to "Go and do the same" (Luke 10:37 NLT).

Always on the *go*...

In our daily lives it is interesting how many places we 'go'. We go to work, go to school, go shopping, go on vacation, go out to eat, go to sporting events, go to the movies, go to the doctor, and go to church.

As believers, His Spirit is in us and therefore with us wherever we go. Some people feel led to go to a foreign mission field. I believe wherever you are right now can be a mission field and the perfect place to do what God asks all of us to do when we go…love others.

The theme of love holds an unparalleled high degree of significance in Jesus' ministry. It is so important He refers to loving God and loving others as the greatest commandment.

You've lost that loving feeling. It can be a challenge to grasp what love means. Our world tends to define love as a feeling, which like happiness, is temporary and depends on the situation. The kind of love Jesus shared and showed is deeper than just feelings. It is a love that loves forgivingly, unconditionally, and sacrificially.

Confusion about the transfusion.

Relating to sacrificial love, I'm reminded of the true story in the first *Chicken Soup for the Soul* book by Jack Canfield about a little girl named Liza who was suffering from a rare and serious disease. Her only chance of survival was a blood transfusion from her five-year-old brother who had miraculously survived the same disease.

The doctor explained the situation to her younger brother and asked if he would be willing to give his blood to his sister. Her brother agreed that he would if it would save Liza's life.

He lay in the bed next to her and smiled as the transfusion progressed and the color miraculously returned to her cheeks. Then his face grew pale, and his smile faded. He looked up at the doctor and with a trembling voice asked, "Will I start to die right away?"

He misunderstood the doctor and thought he would have to give her *all* his blood. But he loved his sister so much he was literally willing to give his life so she could live—just as Christ did for us. Pause and let that thought marinate a moment.

It's *your* move... *your* turn!

Growing up my mom loved to play the board game *SORRY*. I still enjoy playing a competitive game of *UNO* with our family.

In both situations it's usually just a matter of time before everyone is looking at and waiting on me with someone eventually sharing, "It's *your* turn!"

It's time to transition from *reading* about the Good News to *doing*. Time to 'stop talking the talk' and 'start walking the walk'. Time to stop just reading *about* love and start *going, giving,* and *living* love.

How? Just start with something simple like looking for at least one opportunity each day to 'pay it forward' with one act of love and kindness—expecting nothing in return. It's about making a personal commitment to demonstrate God's love.

I encourage you to prayerfully read the following personal declaration:

Go, Show and Share God's Unlimited Love!

The decision has been made. I've stepped over the line. I will stop being a fan of His and start being a follower. I won't look back, let up, slow down, back away or be still. I am finished and done with sight-walking, mundane talking, small-planning, colorless-dreams, tame-visions, and dwarfed-goals.

I no longer need preeminence, prosperity, positions, promotions, plaudits, or popularity. I don't have to be right, recognized, rewarded, or regarded. I now live by prayer and presence, lean by faith, love by patience, and labor by power.

I will not flinch in the face of sacrifice, hesitate in the presence of adversity, ponder at the pool of popularity, or meander in the maze of mediocrity.

I will not give up, let up, or slow up, until I've prayed up, paid up, stored up, and stayed up for the cause of Christ!

Start Living Life Out Loud!

It can be a little overwhelming to step over the line and commit to loving people and share the Good News where they are. Sometimes we need to be reminded that we can find specific encouraging words in His Word to help us as we travel along our personal faith journey. Some powerful promises to help during tough times:

- When you are discouraged, scared, lack confidence, or feel like giving up, "Be strong and courageous. Do not be afraid; do not be discouraged, for the LORD your God will be with you wherever you go" (Joshua 1:9 NIV).
- When you feel tired, bored, or burned out from doing the 'same old, same old' in life, "I am about to do something new. See, I have already begun" (Isaiah 43:19 NLT).
- When you are worried and anxious and need assurance that God cares about you, "Give all your worries and cares to God, for He cares about you" (1 Peter 5:7 NLT).

Now It's Time for YOU To "GO!"

God may possibly put you in situations or send you places for which you don't feel qualified to go. Remember, *God doesn't call the qualified, He qualifies the called.* Or He may want you to stay where you are but now wants you to go there with a transformed, loving heart. Remember:

> We can't spell 'GOD' without the word GO.
> We can't spell 'GOSPEL' without the word GO.
> We can't spell 'GOOD NEWS' without the word GO.

Go…Every Day and Unleash the Unlimited Love of the Good News with the People in Your World and Start Living Life Out Loud!

Positive Points to Ponder
- You can never *go* wrong when you choose to follow Him. He promises to *go* with you and make the crooked paths in your journey straight. And wherever you are *going*–He is already there!
- Jesus did not invite most of us to become theologians or Bible Scholars. He did not call us to be more religious. He did not ask us to join a club or a committee. He invites us to begin an amazing journey of sharing and showing the Good News of God's love with three simple, life-changing words: **"Come, follow Me!"**

Digging Deeper
Small Group Study Guide

This Small Group Study Guide can help your small group, or you, gain a better understanding of the scriptures and *Good News You Can Use*. Plus, you will enjoy the fellowship as you learn together.

Reading the Bible can be difficult and confusing, but it doesn't need to be. Because of its ease and simplicity to use, the *SOAP Method* is one of the most popular methods utilized by individuals or groups. It does not require an extensive degree of Biblical knowledge or special leadership skills. Follow this simple method and feel free to utilize iphones or electronic media during the discussion for each session.

Scripture—Read the main scripture passage out loud from the Bible. This is stated beside the heading *Snapshot Picture of Scripture* in each chapter of the book. Most of these are brief and for the few that may be a little longer, refer to the paraphrased paragraphs right below the heading.

Observation—Who are the main characters and what can you find out about them? Who is speaking? Where does it take place? What stands out in the passage to you? What does this passage or verse tell you about God or Jesus? What does it tell you about humanity (or yourself)?

Application—How can you apply something from this passage to your life? Read, share, and discuss some of the main points or highlights mentioned throughout the chapter in the book. Was there a thought or insight that you could relate to? Anything specific that you can apply to a current situation in your life?

Prayer—Thank God and express gratitude for what you've learned from his Word, the book, and others in the group. Ask Him to help you apply it to your life. *Pray at the beginning and end of each session.* During your ending prayer you might consider using the 'Sandwich Model'. Always begin prayer expressing gratitude, follow with needs and requests and end with gratitude and praise.

Note: Before beginning this study, it is highly recommended to watch the short video, 'How to S.O.A.P.' It quickly explains how to use this simple method of reading and studying the scriptures. (Source: my.salvos.org.au) Click on "toolkit" and type S.O.A.P. in the "Search" bar.

Helpful Hints to Make Your Sessions Prime Time:

Every group is different. Some like to provide food or BYOS–Bring Your Own Snacks. Others leave it up to each individual.

If your group is new, the leader and participants should share and agree on a few basic guidelines to make the best use of your time possible. With busy schedules people appreciate respecting their time and are more likely to attend regularly when it is *typically scheduled for 60 or a maximum of 90 minutes*. Whatever you decide–stick to it.

Bring a Bible (physical or electronic) and a copy of the book to each session. Ever tried to assemble something with a lot of parts without the instructions? The same is true for reading or studying without the resource. As you read and discuss the book feel free to highlight or make notes in the margins for personal future reference.

Rethink and Readjust the 'Round Robin'. In a sincere effort to engage everyone, many times a leader will ask participants to go around a table or circle one-by-one to pray, share requests, read out loud or answer questions. Keep in mind that not everyone feels comfortable or wants to say something every time. If things become a little quiet, maybe it's simply time to move on.

Celebrate and Enjoy! The days Jesus was physically on earth, He and His disciples continued to follow God's command and celebrated seven special festivals or feasts every year. Somewhere we dropped the ball on the importance of celebrating. Be creative. It is appropriate, important, and suggested to plan a few minutes at a study session every so often to fellowship, show gratitude for the goodness of God, and CELEBRATE!

Gratitude

Joanne Liggan - In addition to your invaluable help as a professional author, consultant, editor, Biblical pundit, and project manager, you became a much-needed encourager and prayer partner. Without your assistance and leadership, this book project would not have become a reality! (https://biblestudyFACTS.info)

Heather Heckel - Your gifts, talents, and creative technology skills as a graphic artist in designing the book cover were awesome. (ramblingstarpublishing@gmail.com)

Skip Brown - Your experience and expertise as a recording engineer and producer for the audiobook made the waiting worth it. You are the best of the best and the facilities at Final Track Studios is state of the art. (https://finaltrackstudios.com)

Personal - Friends, former colleagues, pastors and mentors - your personal relationships and life-lessons mean more than you can know. I am blessed to know and learn from each of you.

My Family - Jon and Chris - you both make me such a proud dad as you demonstrate daily your faith as loving fathers and husbands.
Angelee and Morgann - my wonderful daughters-in-love - and captivating grandchildren - Samson, Malachi, Anderson, Carson, and Sienna - all of you remind me to live a life full of God's love and lots of laughter!

My Heavenly Father - You are the One who sacrificed your only Son, the Christ, who brought us the Good News and made it possible to live a life of abundant love!

Bibliography
Sources and Notes

Scripture verses marked NKJV are taken from the New King James Version. Copyright c 1982 by Thomas Nelson, Inc. Used by permission. All rights reserved.

Scripture verses marked NIV are taken from the HOLY BIBLE, NEW INTERNATIONAL VERSION r. NIV r. Copyright c 1973, 1978, 1984, 2011, by the International Bible Society. Used by permission of Zondervan. All rights reserved.

Scripture verses marked NRSV are from the New Revised Standard Version of the Bible, copyright c 1989 by the Division of Christian Education of the National Council of the churches of Christ in the USA. Used by permission. All rights reserved.

Scripture verses marked NASB are taken from the New American Standard Bible r, c 1960, 1962, 1963, 1968, 1071, 1972, 1973, 1975, 1977, 1995 by The Lockman Foundation. Used by permission. (www.Lockman.org)

Scripture verses marked MSG are taken from The Message. Copyright c
by Eugene H. Peterson 1993, 1994, 1995, 1996, 2000, 2001, 2002. Used by permission of NavPress Publishing Group.

Scripture verses marked NLT are taken from the *Holy Bible*, New Living Translation, copyright c 1996, 2004. Used by permission of Tyndale House Publishers, Inc., Wheaton, IL 60189 USA. All rights reserved.

Scripture verses marked ESV are from the Holy Bible, English Standard Version, copyright c 2001 by Crossway Bibles, a division of

Good News Publishers. Used by permission. All rights reserved.
The Case for Miracles: A Journalist Investigates Evidence for the Supernatural, Lee Strobel, Zondervan, 2018

The Problem of Pain, C. S. Lewis, HarperCollins, 1940

Liar, Lord or Lunatic?, C. S. Lewis, published in *Mere Christianity, 1952.*

A Meal with Jesus, Tim Chester, Crossway Publishing, 2011.

Science Speaks: An Evaluation of Certain Christian Evidences, P. W. Stoner and R. C. Newman, Abebooks, 1952.

Handbook of Christian Apologetics, Peter Kreeft and Ronald K. Tacelli, InterVarsity Press, 1994.

Jesus: The God Who Knows Your Name, Max Lucado, Thomas Nelson, 2020.

52 Weeks Through the Bible, James Merritt, Harvest House, 2014

Good to Great, Jim C. Collins, HarperBusiness, 2001.

The Purpose Driven Life, Rick Warren, Zondervan, 2002.

In A Pit with A Lion On A Snowy Day: How to Survive and Thrive, Mark Batterson, The Crown Publishing Group, 2016.

F.A.C.T.S. **F**aith **A**nd **C**ommitment **T**hrough **S**cripture: *A New Testament Bible Study Series,* Joanne Liggan, www.liggan.net, 2021.

Don't Sweat the Small Stuff, Richard Carlson, Hyperion, 1997.

Refocus: Living a Life That Reflects God's Heart, Zondervan, *2012.*

Would Jesus Wear a Rolex, Chet Atkins, Margaret Archer, Ray Stevens, Universal Music Group, 1987.

Life Without Limits: Inspiration for a Ridiculously Good Life, Nick Vujicic,

Allen & Unwin, 2012.

When God Winks, Squire Rushnell, Howard, 2018.

Mission Possible: Daily Devotional, Tim Tebow, Waterbrook, Tim Tebow Foundation, 2022

DiSC Biblical Personal Profile System, William M. Marston, John Geier, Insight Publishing, 1970.

A View From the Zoo, Gary Richmond, DMJ Media Group, 2005.

It's Hard to Be Humble, Mac Davis, Casablanca, 1974.

Preach It, Teach It, Dr. Roger Barrier, Crosswalk.com.

A Long Walk to Freedom, Nelson Mandella, MacDonald Purnell, 1994.

Jesus! Jesus! Jesus! There's Just Something About That Name, Bill Gaither and Gloria Gaither, 1970, hymnary.org.

It Is Well with My Soul, Horatio Spafford, Published Gospel Hymns No. 2, 1876.

Judge Softly, Mary T. Lathrap, 1895

Amazing Grace, John Newton, written 1772, published 1779.

Praise You In the Storm, Bernie Herms and Mark Hall, Beach Street and Reunion, Casting Crowns, 2006.

The Laughing Jesus, Willis Wheatley, 1973.

Gallup Poll, Church Attendance, 2023

A Deeper Faith: Nurture Your Relationship with God and Live a Faith-Fueled Life, Pamela L. Palmer, Typewriter Creative Co., 2022, www.upheldlife.com, www.biblestudytools.com, www.HerViewFromHome.com

That's My King, Rev. Dr. S. M. Lockridge, revpacman.co.

canonjjohn.com, John Loannou, Philo Trust, 1982

10 Surprising Lessons from the Parable of the Good Samaritan, www.becoming christians.org.

The Bible Book: Big Ideas Simply Explained, Penguin Random House, DK Books, Doering Kindersley Limited, 2015.

A Hiding Place, Corrie Ten Boom, Bernadette Dunne, Baker Publishing Group, 2010.

Lessons I Learned in the Dark, Jennifer Rothschild, Multnomah Publisher, 2002.

www.learningreligions.org

www.gotquestions.org

www.kindspring.org

www.belief.net

www.hegetsus.com

Good News You Can Use can be purchased as an e-book, audiobook, or paperback at Amazon.com.

Author Jerry King welcomes hearing from readers. Contact him via e-mail at jerryking8184@gmail.com.

NOTES & QUOTES
(Please use these pages for your own notes.)

NOTES & QUOTES

NOTES & QUOTES

Made in the USA
Columbia, SC
11 June 2025